C.S. LEWIS

Images of His World

C.S. LEWIS
Images of His World

DOUGLAS GILBERT
CLYDE S. KILBY

WILLIAM B. EERDMANS PUBLISHING COMPANY
Grand Rapids, Michigan

Fourth Reprinting, November 1979

Library of Congress Cataloging in Publication Data

Gilbert, Douglas, 1942–
C. S. Lewis: images of his world.

1. Lewis, Clive Staples, 1898–1963. I. Kilby, Clyde S. I. Title.
PR6023.E926Z66   828'.9'1209 [B]   73-8697
ISBN 0-8028-1545-6

Printed in the United States of America.

The authors are grateful for permission to quote from the following
books by C. S. Lewis:
The Four Loves, © 1960 by Helen Joy Lewis. By permission of Har-
court Brace Jovanovich.
The Horse and His Boy, Copyright, 1954, by The Macmillan Com-
pany and © C. S. Lewis 1954. By permission of The Macmillan
Company and Collins, Sons, and Company, Ltd.
The Letters of C. S. Lewis, Copyright © 1966 by W. H. Lewis and
Executors of C. S. Lewis. By permission of Harcourt Brace Jovano-
vich and of Collins, Sons, and Company, Ltd.
Letters to Malcolm: Chiefly on Prayer, © 1963, 1964 by the Estate
of C. S. Lewis and/or C. S. Lewis. By permission of Harcourt Brace
Jovanovich and of Collins, Sons, and Company, Ltd.
The Lion, the Witch and the Wardrobe, Copyright, 1950, by the
Macmillan Company and © C. S. Lewis, 1950. By permission of the
Macmillan Company and Collins, Sons, and Company, Ltd.
The Magician's Nephew, Copyright, 1955, by C. S. Lewis and ©

C. S. Lewis 1958. By permission of The Macmillan Company and
The Bodley Head Ltd.
Of Other Worlds, © The Executors of the Estate of C. S. Lewis, 1966.
By permission of Harcourt Brace Jovanovich and of Collins, Sons,
and Company, Ltd.
Out of the Silent Planet, by permission of The Macmillan Company
and The Bodley Head Ltd.
Prince Caspian, Copyright, 1951, by The Macmillan Company. By
permission of The Macmillan Company and Collins, Sons, and
Company, Ltd.
Reflections on the Psalms, © C. S. Lewis, 1958. By permission of Har-
court Brace Jovanovich and of Collins, Sons, and Company, Ltd.
Surprised by Joy, © Copyright, 1955, by C. S. Lewis. By permission of
Harcourt Brace Jovanovich and of Collins, Sons, and Company, Ltd.
Permission has also been granted to quote from *Light on C. S. Lewis,*
ed. Jocelyn Gibb, © Geoffrey Bles Ltd., 1965. Permission by Har-
ccurt Brace Jovanovich and by Collins, Sons, and Company, Ltd.

Contents

Introduction

A decade after C. S. Lewis's death, all of the more than fifty titles that have been published under his name are in print except his first collection of lyric poetry, *Spirits in Bondage*. As the works of scholarly, creative, and theological contemporaries once better known than he drop out of sight, Lewis's works seem to be attracting ever wider attention.

There are many facets to the appeal of C. S. Lewis. Some readers, especially children, find the *Narnia* tales among the most captivating books they have ever read. College students may reserve their greatest appreciation for his science fiction trilogy. His well-known studies in literary criticism are gaining increasing use as standard textbooks. Many Christian readers have found strength from reading his apologetic writings, whose clarity and concision have won the praise even of those who cannot confess the faith behind them.

A self-confessed romantic, Lewis was probably one of the most realistic writers of his day. He was an author, wrote Charles A. Brady, whose veins "run blood, not ink. There is no mildew in his bones nor mere jargon on his lips." Testimonies from Lewis readers verify that. For many his writings have had an effect that marks him as far more than just another author. He is the kind of writer who can usher the reader into a new world, into a continuing process of discovery that reconstitutes his way of thought and life. Said one college student after reading Lewis: "Even the little ideas are shattering in their implications and set my thoughts reverberating as if to a cymbal clashing." Another admitted, "I never before realized that the supernatural world was a reality . . . that God is so big." A professor of history at a college in Virginia wrote, "C. S. Lewis was one of the mainstays during the crisis of my wife's death and the grief afterwards." A class of youngsters with brain damage was introduced to Lewis's *Narnia* tales, and their teacher found them for the first time intensely interested in a book.

Our purpose in what follows is to offer a portrait of C. S. Lewis and the milieu in which he lived. Using words and pictures, we have tried to represent vividly some aspects of his life. Archaeologists prefer evidence they can study *in situ* — against the backdrop of the world in which it flourished. So, too, we want in this book to look at Lewis *in situ:* the little boy in Ireland already displaying unusual talents in writing and drawing, the youth crossing the Irish Sea to attend school in England, the university teacher at Magdalen College in Oxford and Magdalene College in Cambridge. We wish to show the much-loved deer park outside his rooms at Magdalen, the Kilns where he spent most of his life, the places he walked and swam and talked. In the process we shall introduce some of his closest friends and colleagues.

The subtitle "Images of His World" describes our focus. We have not meant to put together a travelogue. Undoubtedly, the subjects of many of these photographs would be worthy items on the agenda for a holiday in the British Isles; but our emphasis has been on recapturing what Lewis saw. Nor, on the other hand, have we aimed to produce an interpretive biography of Lewis. There is, for reference, a chronological account of the important dates of his life under the heading "Biography in Little." The longer essay "From Atheist to Christian" seeks to interpret his central religious and intellectual pilgrimage, a spiritual journey that is essential to understanding Lewis the Christian writer whose influence we have referred to above. "Lewis struck me as the most thoroughly *converted* man I ever met," Father Walter Hooper has written. "His whole vision of life was such that the natural and supernatural seemed inseparably combined." So it is that an awareness of the long and difficult process by which Lewis became a believer in Christ aids in grasping the images of his world.

The list of people to whom we incurred obligations in the preparation of this book is long. First of all we should mention those who cooperated in the taking of thousands of photographs, a relative few of which are presented here. Particular gratitude is due the late Major W. H. Lewis, who allowed us to photograph not only the outside and inside of the Kilns, but also a number of family pictures and the boyhood manuscripts of his brother. Father Hooper also graciously allowed Mr. Gilbert to photograph the memorial gathering in the summer of 1972.

We owe special thanks to Colin Hardie, Lewis's friend and colleague at Magdalen; and to Dr. Robert Havard for his account of a walking trip with Lewis in Wales; and to Wroxton College for permission to photograph Lewis's library. We are grateful to Pauline Baynes for the privilege of reproducing two of her Narnia drawings, and to Mr. Jocelyn Gibb for his words about Lewis in relation to his publisher.

We were eager to let Lewis's own words describe some of the photographs. We are most grateful that the Lewis Estate granted permission to use excerpts from some hitherto unpublished writings of Lewis, especially from his letters to Arthur Greeves. For specific quotations we express our thanks to Harcourt Brace Jovanovich, The Macmillan Company, Collins, Sons, and Company, Ltd., The Bodley Head Ltd., Cambridge University Press, Henry Z. Walck, Inc., and the Wm. B. Eerdmans Publishing Company. Specific sources of quotations from books by these publishers are found on page 192.

We thank also the *London Observer* for the picture of Lewis and Joy on page 64, the Bodleian Library for the map of Narnia by Lewis on page 15, Mr. Raymond Hunt for the picture of Charles Williams on p. 48, Mr. F. W. Paxford for pictures of The Kilns and for the photograph of Mrs. Jane King Moore on page 11, Mr. and Mrs. Len Miller for the picture of Lewis on page 10, and Miss Cathy Cody for excerpts used from a paper she wrote on Lewis's interest in the natural world.

Our thanks should also go to Stephen Schofield of Surrey for help in locating some dates in the chronology of Lewis and for being the longtime friend of our work. Significant friends also are Mr. and Mrs. Len Miller.

Particular thanks are due Mr. Alan Sorrell for use of the painting of Lewis and some of his friends at Magdalen College. We also want to thank Owen Barfield for good-naturedly supplying the cartoons appearing on page 45.

And, by no means least, thanks go to Barbara Gilbert and Martha Kilby. Barbara was particularly involved in developing the concept of the book and attending to many details in caption writing and layout.

DOUGLAS GILBERT

Wheaton, Illinois   CLYDE S. KILBY

BIOGRAPHY IN LITTLE

November 29, 1898. Clive Staples Lewis was born in Belfast, Ireland, the second of two sons of Albert James Lewis, a solicitor, and Flora Augusta Hamilton Lewis. His brother Warren, three years older, remarked later that the childhood years of the two boys laid "the foundations of an intimate friendship that was the greatest happiness of my life."

1905. The Lewis family moved to "Little Lea," a large new house. "I am the product," he wrote later, "of long corridors, empty sunlit rooms, upstair indoor silences, attics explored in solitude . . . also of endless books." In good weather the two brothers explored County Down on their bicycles. Early in his childhood Lewis experienced a feeling of *Sehnsucht,* a deep-seated longing for Joy that was not to be fulfilled until 1929 in his submission to God. Even before he could write, little "Jacksie" (as he asked to be called) was making up stories, which his father would write down for him. He was also writing verses at a very early age.

August 23, 1908. Flora Lewis died of cancer. The rearing of the children had been nominally Christian, and the young Lewis prayed to the "magician" God to keep his mother alive. When she died, he wanted Him to go away.

September 1908 (to 1910). The two brothers went off to England to school at Wynyard ("Belsen"), in Watford, Hertfordshire. It was a miserable experience. Shortly afterwards the school closed, and the often brutal headmaster was declared insane. But it was here that Lewis first heard Christianity taught in its simple directness. He began seriously to pray and read the Bible.

Autumn 1910. For half a term Lewis attended Campbell College, near his home in Ireland. He left because of illness and his father's dissatisfaction with the school.

January 1911 (to summer of 1913). Lewis returned to England and Cherbourg House ("Chartres"), a preparatory school in Malvern. His brother was in Malvern College ("Wyvern") at the same time. By now he had begun to love England. A number of important developments transpired during this period. He "ceased to be a Christian," learned to wear flashy clothes and practice fornication, and discovered a copy of *Siegfried and the Twilight of the Gods* and Wagner's music, which brought back like a flood his earlier romantic longings. He began to write an heroic poem on the Nibelung epic and also created his stories of the political history of Boxen, including "The Life of Lord John Big of Bigham," Lord Big being a frog.

September 1913 (to July 1914). After winning a classical scholarship, he entered Malvern College. Within a few weeks he gained attention with a brilliant translation of Horace. Here also he worked on his "Loki Bound," a tragedy in Greek form about Norse gods, atheistic and pessimistic in tone. "I maintained that God did not exist. I was also very angry with God for not existing. I was equally angry with Him for creating a world." He came slowly to hate this school and persuaded his father to remove him.

Spring 1914. Lewis met and became the lifelong friend of Joseph Arthur Greeves, another lover of "Northernness." Their correspondence was to last for forty-nine years.

September 1914 (to 1916). For two years Lewis studied with the ruthless dialectician W. T. Kirkpatrick ("the Great Knock"), who prepared him for entrance to Oxford. Lewis was extremely happy with his freedom, including, as the atheistic student of an atheistic tutor, his freedom from God. He loved to walk through the countryside and was overjoyed at his progress in learning Greek, Latin, French, German, and Italian. He did extensive reading in English and American literature and listened often to great music. He also wrote a good deal, including lyrical poetry and a romance or two in prose.

October 1915. Reading George MacDonald's *Phantastes* introduced a new quality into his life, which later he identified as "holiness." The book, he said, "baptised" his imagination.

December 1916. He sat for a classical scholarship at Oxford and was elected to University College. He wrote his father, "This place has surpassed my wildest dreams; I never saw anything so beautiful."

January 1917 (to March). Lewis continued to study under Kirkpatrick for Responsions, but failed because of his inability in mathematics.

April 28, 1917. He began his studies at Oxford, but before the term ended he was recruited into the army, the Great War being then in its crescendo. In the billets at Keble College, Oxford, his roommate was the Irishman E. F. C. ("Paddy") Moore. Lewis also became acquainted with Paddy's mother, Mrs. Janie King Moore. Paddy Moore was killed in the war, and Lewis became a son to the widowed Mrs. Moore — a relationship that was to continue to her death in 1951 — and brother to Maureen Moore (now Lady Dunbar of Hempriggs and wife of Leonard Blake).

September 25, 1917. Commissioned as Second Lieutenant in the Somerset Light Infantry in September, Lewis embarked for France two months later, arriving in the front lines on his nineteenth birthday. He thanked Arthur Greeves for writing to Mrs. Moore, who was then in France. Lewis was glad that "the two people who mean most to me in the world are in touch."

C. S. Lewis,
July, 1919

1918. In January Lewis was hospitalized in the British Red Cross Hospital at Le Tréport, suffering from trench fever. Though glad to be away from the battle front, he was convinced that ". . . the gods hate me — and naturally enough considering my usual attitude towards them." He rejoined his battalion on March 4, but was wounded in action at Mount Bernenchon, near Lilliers, and hospitalized on April 14.

May 22, 1918. Lewis was returned to "a vastly comfortable hospital" in England. The pieces of shrapnel in his chest gave him no serious trouble. He made light of the fact that he had brought in about sixty German soldiers as prisoners. During his hospitalization, and even while in the trenches, he had never ceased his wide reading, including Milton, Scott, Trollope, Boswell, George Eliot, Cellini, and Balzac.

June 16, 1918. Out of the hospital, Lewis visited the Kirkpatricks at Great Bookham. "I opened the gate of Kirk's garden almost with stealth, and went on past the house to the vegetable garden and the little wild orchard with the pond where I had sat so often on hot Sunday afternoons, and there among the cabbages in his shirt and Sunday trousers, sure enough was the old man, still digging and smoking his horrible pipe. . . . I was led into the house with much triumph and displayed to Mrs. Kirk, whom we found fussing with the maid, just as old. I have seldom spent a more delightful afternoon."

January 1919. About his return to University College, Oxford, Lewis wrote, "The place is looking more beautiful than ever in the wintry frost; one gets splendid cold colouring at the expense of tingling fingers and red noses." He began to make many lifelong friends, including Owen Barfield, "wisest and best of my unofficial teachers," who was then a student at Wadham College.

1919. Lewis published *Spirits in Bondage*, his first book, a small volume of lyric poems, under the pen name of Clive Hamilton.* Concerning the book he wrote his father: "This little success gives me a pleasure which is perhaps childish, and yet akin to

*Only books are listed in this biography. Lewis also published many essays, prefaces, book reviews, and poems, and two short stories.

greater things." The main theme, he later said, was that "nature is wholly diabolical and malevolent and that God, if he exists, is outside and in opposition to the cosmic arrangement." The book received a few short reviews of little consequence.

Spring 1920. Took a First in Honor Mods.

March 14, 1921. Made his first visit to the home of William Butler Yeats.

April 1922. Began the composition of *Dymer,* a long narrative poem. During this year he also began a verse version of *Till We Have Faces.*

1922. Took a First in Greats.

1923. Took a First in English and won the Chancellor's Prize for an English essay. Throughout his undergraduate career Lewis continued to write, especially narrative poetry, much of which he destroyed.

March 1924. At the end of his first year at Oxford Lewis had established a home for Mrs. Moore. One brief entry in his journal describes his situation then. "During this time it was unfortunate that my first spring flood of *Dymer* should co-incide with a burst of marmalade-making and spring-cleaning on Mrs. Moore's part, which led without intermission into packing. I managed to get through a good deal of writing in the intervals of jobbing in the kitchen and doing messages. . . . I also kept my temper nearly all the time. Domestic drudgery is excellent as an alternative to idleness or to hateful thoughts — which is perhaps poor Mrs. Moore's reason for piling it on all the time; as an alternative to the work one is longing to do and able to do (*at that time* and heaven knows when again) it is maddening. No one's fault; the curse of Adam."

October 1924. Lewis began tutorial work at University College, replacing E. F. Carritt, philosophy tutor, for one year.

May 1925. Elected to a Fellowship in English Language and Literature at Magdalen College, Oxford, where he was to remain until 1954. Lewis began to tutor, lecture, and set and grade examinations. Though not greatly impressed with the

quality of all his pupils, he was happy to have a fixed income. His college rooms were splendidly located above the famous deer park, and within a minute of sitting at his desk he could be stretching his legs down Addison's Walk and beside the Cherwell. About this time his friends included a number of persons who were later to be members of the Inklings — among them J. R. R. Tolkien, Nevill Coghill, H. V. D. Dyson, and A. C. Harwood. His day usually included a visit to his home, at first in Headington and later at The Kilns in Headington Quarry, about three miles east of Magdalen, where he had lunch, took the dogs for a walk over Shotover Hill, helped Mrs. Moore can pears, plums, apples, cherries, and such, and often in warm weather went for a swim in the pond between the house and the timbered hill that he owned and loved.

1926. Again using the pen name Clive Hamilton, Lewis published his book-length narrative poem *Dymer,* "the story of a

Mrs. Moore

man who, on some mysterious bride, begets a monster: which monster, since it has killed its father, becomes a god." He said that this story "arrived, complete, in my mind somewhere about my seventeenth year."

Trinity Term 1929. After many years of slowly moving towards Christianity (as detailed in the accompanying essay), he now confessed on his knees in his rooms at Magdalen that "God is God." It was two years later that he and his brother set out by motorcycle for a visit to Whipsnade Zoo, about thirty miles east of Oxford. "When we set out I did not believe that Jesus Christ is the Son of God, and when we reached the zoo I did."

September 1929. A. J. Lewis died in Belfast. Since Warren was in China, Clive arranged his father's funeral and settled the estate. During his father's last illness, he would put him to bed and go out and walk in the garden, sometimes having a long talk with his boyhood friend Arthur Greeves. "Every room," he wrote Owen Barfield, "is soaked with the bogeys of childhood — the awful 'rows' with my father, the awful returnings to school, and also with the old pleasures of an unusually ignoble adolescence." At the same time Lewis showed a genuine appreciation of many of his father's good qualities.

October 1930. Lewis and the Moores settled at The Kilns, the house in which he was thereafter to live. Before long his brother came there to live, and a wing was added to the house. Major Lewis became an authority on early seventeenth-century French history and published several books.

1933. *The Pilgrim's Regress: An Allegorical Apology for Christianity, Reason and Romanticism* was published, a fictionalized autobiography in which a boy, having tasted Joy, goes on a long journey to find it again and discovers that he might have had it with less effort near home. In a later edition, Lewis summarized its theme: ". . . if a man diligently followed his desire [for Joy], pursuing the false objects until their falsity appeared and then resolutely abandoned them, he must come out at last into the clear knowledge that the human soul was made to enjoy some object that is never fully given . . . in our present mode of subjective and spatio-temporal existence."

1936. Lewis published *The Allegory of Love: A Study in Medieval Tradition.* This study earned him a wide reputation as a scholar and won him the Hawthornden Prize. Said Professor Ifor Evans in the *Observer:* "Out of the multitude of volumes on literary criticism there arises once or twice in a generation a truly great work. Such, I believe, is this study." Shortly after publication of *The Allegory,* Lewis and Charles Williams, the author of many books, began the correspondence which led to their close friendship.

1937. Won Gollancz Memorial Prize.

1938. *Out of the Silent Planet* appeared, a novel telling of a spaceship carrying two evil men and a Christian to Mars and describing their adventures there among odd-looking but intelligent and splendid creatures.

1939. Published *The Personal Heresy: A Controversy,* a debate with E. M. W. Tillyard, Master of Jesus College, Cambridge, on whether poetry should be the expression of the poet's personality. Lewis held to the belief that poetry should be objective and impersonal.

September 1939. Charles Williams moved to Oxford, when the Oxford University Press, where he worked, was forced to move from London with the onset of World War II. The two were close friends until Williams's death on May 15, 1945. Afterward, Lewis described him as ". . . my friend of friends, the comforter of all our little set, the most angelic man" and said that his death gave "a corroboration to my belief in immortality such as I never dreamed of — it is almost tangible now."

1939. Lewis published *Rehabilitations and Other Essays,* a collection of studies of English writers, of British education, and similar topics.

1940. Published *The Problem of Pain,* which C. E. M. Joad of the University of London called "the most elaborate and careful account" known to him on the subject.

1940 through 1941. Lewis served as wartime lecturer on Christianity for the Royal Air Force.

1941. He helped form the Socratic Club at Oxford, of which he was longtime president.

August 6, 1941. Began his first twenty-five talks over the British Broadcasting Corporation radio.

1942. Published *Broadcast Talks: Reprinted with Some Alterations from Two Series of Broadcast Talks ('Right and Wrong: A Clue to the Meaning of the Universe' and 'What Christians Believe') Given in 1941 and 1942.* Later revised, these form the first two portions of *Mere Christianity.*

1942. Published *The Screwtape Letters,* his most popular book but in his opinion not at all his best. It portrays the devil's view of Christian conduct and how hell seeks to circumvent goodness. From the proceeds of this book a charitable trust was established, and two-thirds of all Lewis's royalties thereafter went into it. The same year saw the appearance of *A Preface to 'Paradise Lost', Being the Ballard Matthews Lectures Delivered at University College, North Wales.* The *New Statesman* called this book "a delight for all who must for ever love Milton . . . a brilliant link in a long chain which is a credit to English thought."

Left to right:
Commander Dundas-Grant, Colin Hardie, Dr. Robert Havard, C. S. Lewis, Peter Havard

1943. Published *Christian Behaviour: A Further Series of Broadcast Talks.* Later, in revised form, this became the third portion of *Mere Christianity.* Also, he published *Perelandra,* the account of a voyage to the unfallen planet of Venus by a Christian and a devil-possessed man. Each attempts to persuade the "Eve" there of his point of view, and the Christian is at last successful. A third publication was *The Abolition of Man, or Reflections on Education with Special Reference to the Teaching of English in the Upper Forms of Schools,* three lectures given at Durham University, which consider whether man will deny the moral and supernatural order in favor of private notions.

1944. Published *Beyond Personality: The Christian Idea of God,* talks over BBC later revised and issued as the last portion of *Mere Christianity.*

1945. Published *That Hideous Strength: A Modern Fairy-Story for Grown-ups,* the last volume in the trilogy including *Out of the Silent Planet* and *Perelandra.* It is a story of men intent on refashioning society after their private notions and finally turning man into God. Also *The Great Divorce: A Dream* appeared. In this book a busload of people in hell go on an excursion to the outskirts of heaven. Though they are warmly encouraged to enter, with one exception they refuse the offer.

1946. Lewis was awarded the Doctorate of Divinity by St. Andrews University, and published *George MacDonald: An Anthology,* a tribute to the Scottish writer who probably had a greater influence on Lewis than any other author.

1947. Published *Miracles: A Preliminary Study.* Lewis considers whether miracles are possible and, if so, how they interlock with the natural world.

1948. Published *Arthurian Torso: Containing the Posthumous Fragment of "The Figure of Arthur" by Charles Williams and a Commentary on the Arthurian Poems of Charles Williams by C. S. Lewis.*

1949. Published *Transposition and Other Addresses,* a collection of some of Lewis's finest essays. (The American title is *The Weight of Glory and Other Addresses.*)

1950. Published *The Lion, the Witch and the Wardrobe,* the first of seven Narnia stories. In this one Aslan (Christ) dies in order to redeem a traitorous boy from death.

1951. Published *Prince Caspian: The Return to Narnia.* The four Pevensie children are whisked by magic to help Prince Caspian overcome many evil enemies.

1951. Lewis was offered the honor of Commander of the Order of the British Empire by the Prime Minister, but cordially refused. Death of Mrs. Jane King Moore, Lewis's "adopted" mother.

September 22, 1952. The Doctorate of Literature was awarded Lewis, *in absentia,* by Laval University, Quebec.

1952. Published *Mere Christianity* and *The Voyage of the 'Dawn Treader.'* In the latter, three children go far eastward on an adventurous sea journey, accompanied by the gallant mouse Reepicheep, who is seeking Aslan's country.

1953. Published *The Silver Chair.* Three children and a Marshwiggle named Puddleglum are finally successful in rescuing Prince Rilian from a beautiful but wicked witch in the far north of Narnia.

1954. Published *The Horse and His Boy.* Two children on talking horses travel from Calormen to Narnia with their journey watched over and directed by the great lion Aslan. Lewis dedicated this book to David and Douglas, the sons of William and Joy Davidman Gresham, whom he was later to marry. A second Lewis publication that year was *English Literature in the Sixteenth Century, Excluding Drama,* originally presented in the Clark Lecture series at Trinity College, Cambridge.

January 1, 1955. After almost thirty years at Oxford, Lewis accepted the Professorship of Medieval and Renaissance Literature at Magdalene College, Cambridge. His inaugural address was entitled *"De Descriptione Temporum."* Dr. G. M. Trevelyan, Master of Trinity at Cambridge, presided for the occasion and later reported that this was, he believed, the only university appointment in which there was a unanimous vote of the elect-

ing committee. Magdalen College at Oxford on his leaving elected him to an Honorary Fellowship.

1955. Lewis published *Surprised by Joy: The Shape of My Early Life,* an autobiography recounting his life up to 1931, and *The Magician's Nephew,* which explains the magical wardrobe by which the children first gained entrance to Narnia, the creation of Narnia by Aslan, and the entrance of evil into it.

1956. Published *The Last Battle.* In this book Narnia comes to its end and the children, with one exception, are taken "further up and further in" to live joyfully with Aslan. This is the seventh and last book to appear in the Narnia series, although Lewis pointed out that these books had no precise order of composition. For this book Lewis was awarded the Carnegie Medal. Also Lewis published *Till We Have Faces: A Myth Retold,* which he regarded as his best book. In it he re-creates the myth of Cupid and Psyche with Christian implications.

C. S. Lewis, walker

April 23, 1956. A legal ceremony united C. S. Lewis in marriage to Joy Davidman Gresham. Both she and her former husband had been very active in the Communist Party in the United States before professing a turn to Christianity as a result of reading the books of Lewis. Lewis and Joy did not actually live together until after a later ecclesiastical marriage in January 1957, at Joy's hospital bed. She had cancer of the thigh. Lewis wrote friends that he might become both husband and widower at the same time. In April 1957, the hospital "sent her home to die," but in June Lewis reported her "to all appearances well." There had been a bedside ceremony of prayer and laying on of hands, and Lewis believed a healing miracle had taken place. The two had a belated honeymoon and returned to live at The Kilns.

1958. Published *Reflections on the Psalms,* containing thoughts to which he found himself driven in reading the Psalms, "some-

times by my enjoyment of them, sometimes by meeting with what at first I could not enjoy."

1960. Published *The Four Loves,* an account of affection, friendship, Eros ("being in love"), and charity, or love of God. He also published *Studies in Words,* lectures given at Cambridge on the words "nature," "sad," "wit," "free," "sense," "simple," and "conscious — conscience." An American publisher brought together seven Lewis essays in *The World's Last Night and Other Essays.*

July 13, 1960. Joy died, about two months after the two had returned from a visit to Greece, an experience she had set her heart on. "The night before she died we had a long, quiet, nourishing, and tranquil talk."

1961. Published *A Grief Observed* under the pen name of N. W. Clerk. It was his outpouring of anguish on the death of his wife Joy. He also published *An Experiment in Criticism,* a book taking issue with many traditional ways of judging literature and proposing a new method.

1962. Published *They Asked for a Paper: Papers and Addresses,* a collection of a dozen essays on such topics as British writers, the Authorized Version of the Bible, psychoanalysis, and literary criticism.

July 1963. Lewis went into a coma and was expected to die. After he recovered he said that he was disappointed not to have been able to enter a door that he saw before him. He resigned his Professorship at Cambridge.

November 22, 1963. C. S. Lewis died at The Kilns from a combination of ailments. He was buried in the churchyard of his parish church, a short distance from The Kilns.

1964. Published, posthumously, *Letters to Malcolm: Chiefly on Prayer.* This was the last book Lewis prepared for the press.

Map of Narnia, by C. S. Lewis

FROM ATHEIST TO CHRISTIAN

After fifteen C. S. Lewis was the happiest he had ever been. His previous schooling had given him pain more often than pleasure. Too many of his schoolmates had displayed every motive but that of real learning. He had grown to hate school sports, especially when he had to take part. He had felt constricted by his father, whom he thought peculiar in his ways and narrow in some of his views. Now he was joyfully immersed in rigorous intellectual training under W. T. Kirkpatrick, "the Great Knock," who was preparing him for entrance to Oxford.

The young Lewis was in love with learning. He had come to love books, not just their contents, but their physical make-up — the quality of their paper, their binding, even their odor. Under his new tutor he had plenty of contact with books. Homer in the original Greek came first, most of the *Iliad* and all of the *Odyssey*. Also Demosthenes, Cicero, Lucretius, Catullus, Tacitus, Herodotus, Euripides, Sophocles, and Virgil. Mrs. Kirkpatrick, the wife of his tutor, had him reading French in the evenings, and he was soon purchasing French books for his own library. A little later came German and Italian, with abundant reading in English and American writers.

Among his new-found freedoms was freedom from God. The fifteen-year-old student was a young atheist being tutored by an older atheist. Lewis had been reared in a nominally Christian home. At one of the schools he had attended he received genuine Christian training, and there he had made serious efforts to practice Christianity. But later circumstances encouraged him to abandon his belief in God, and by fifteen he was calling himself an atheist and writing emphatically of his opposition to God.

During his studies with Kirkpatrick (from 1914 to 1916) Lewis completed a tragedy in Greek form about Norse gods. In it Odin knowingly created a world through wanton cruelty. He had been warned against it but went ahead making creatures simply to vent his anger and spite upon them. Why, the tragedy asked, should the gods, or God, make a world in the first place? A writer of sorts from a very early age, Lewis was now also writing poetry that attacked God and the evil he felt was incarnated in the Ruler of the Universe. If God existed at all, He was more like a demon.

At this period a vigorous correspondence existed between Lewis and his Irish boyhood friend Arthur Greeves. The two had enjoyed many walks and talks together but apparently had never spoken of religion. Now Arthur asked his friend what he thought about religion. Lewis's answer was little less than a tirade. Religion is nothing more than man's own invention and is utterly without real foundation. Primitives made up religion out of their ignorant fears of thunder and other natural phenomena. They came to the point of believing these to be evil spirits and began to try to placate them with sacrifices. Thus various cults arose, usually after the death of a leader. It was out of such a situation that a philosophical Jew called Yeshua, or Jesus, had a cult grow up about him. Lewis rebuked Arthur for being so backward as to fail to join "the educated and thinking" people who ignore such old and decaying superstitions.

Years later Lewis was to put similar arguments in the mouth of an evil witch in his Narnia story *The Silver Chair*. The witch endeavored to persuade the children, who had long been lost underground, that they were wholly mistaken to think that there really was light above them and that such a one as the lion Aslan (Christ) existed. "I see," said the witch, "that we should do no better with your *lion*, as you call it, than we did with your *sun*. You have seen lamps, and so you imagined a better lamp and called it the *sun*. You've seen cats, and now you want a bigger and better cat. . . . Well, it's a pretty make-believe." She almost brought the children under her power before they awakened to her devilish intention.

Arthur asked his friend why with such a negative attitude he did not simply commit suicide. Because, replied Lewis, in spite of fits of occasional depression he was pleased with life and having a good time. Nor did he feel that being an atheist relieved him of all moral responsibility to himself and his community. These are things we owe to our manhood and dignity, quite apart from belief in gods.

Not that Lewis had always strictly followed the morality he postulated. He sometimes lied to his father and even defended the notion that not to lie may itself be criminal. He was quick to curse things he did not like — a guest downstairs, unfavorable weather, fellow pupils — and generally played the fool.

Lewis wrote Arthur that he was willing to look at any new theistic evidences. He conceded that there was indeed "a Hebrew called Yeshua," but "when I say 'Christ' of course I mean the mythological being into whom he was afterwards converted by popular imagination. . . . That the man Yeshua or Jesus did actually exist, is as certain as that the Buddha did actually exist: Tacitus mentions his execution in the Annals. But all the other tomfoolery about virgin birth, magic healings, apparitions and so forth is on exactly the same footing as any other mythology; . . . most legends have a kernel of fact in them somewhere." Arthur suggested in one letter that Lewis was sad simply because he had "no hope of a 'happy life hereafter.'" "No," Lewis wrote back, "strange as it may appear I am quite content to live without believing in a bogey who is prepared to torture me forever . . . a spirit more cruel and barbarous than any man."

How did Lewis turn from such convictions to become one of the most completely orthodox and influential Christians of his generation? From the time of these letters rebuking Greeves to the time of his own conversion was thirteen years. It was a period of indecision in spiritual things. At times he looked back toward atheism; at times forward to a slowly brightening view of Christianity. "It took me as long," he was later to write, "to acquire inhibitions as others (they say) have taken to get rid of them. That is why I often find myself at such cross-purposes with the modern world: I have been a converted Pagan living among apostate Puritans."

Kirkpatrick had helped Lewis prepare for college, and to college he went. Like any other beginner, the scope of his horizon enlarged. He found one fellow who had been an atheist but was turning away from it, and they had a long talk about religion, particularly Buddhism. Another talk ranged over "the rival merits of Swinburne and Keats, the improbability of God,

and Home Rule." He found a girl, "another agnostic" he called her, and they discussed "Christian mythologies." It is often the case that college leads young people away from God. For Lewis, possibly because he had already probed the depth of his unbelief so thoroughly, college contributed to his movement in the other direction.

Lewis continued to read books about religion. Some confirmed his atheism, others disturbed it. He read Berkeley's *Dialogues* and felt that the bishop's efforts to prove the existence of God turned out only to disprove the existence of matter. He read Clutton-Broch's *The Ultimate Belief* and saw that morals might be rooted in God rather than, as he had supposed, in one's accidental convictions of right and wrong.

The next encounter with such ideas was shortly after his entrance to Oxford, when he was sent into the trenches in France, arriving there on his nineteenth birthday. Two periods of leisurely reading were afforded him by a spell of trench fever and a war wound. Several years before, the seed of holiness had been implanted in him when he had sat down on a train and begun to read George MacDonald's *Phantastes*. Now the seed started to bear, if not fruit, at least some foliage. The correspondence with Greeves shows Lewis slowly becoming the occasional defender of spiritual things against his hitherto more orthodox friend.

Arthur had suggested that the beauty of the world is to some degree an evidence of God. From the London hospital where he was recuperating, Lewis took vigorous hold of this idea and pressed it further than Arthur had imagined. Precisely where, he asked, does the beauty of a tree, for example, reside? Like every other physical object, a tree is made up of atoms, and atoms are identical and without color. So when you call a tree beautiful you are actually speaking of something other than the atoms of which it is made. A light from the vibrations in the distant sun produces a wave toward your eye. When it reaches the tissues of your eye another vibration is set up and moves along a nerve like a telegraph wire, carrying the sensation to your brain. One such sensation we call greenness, another brownness, a third shapeliness. But there is no actual color either in the atoms of which the tree is composed or in all those vibrations.

How then does the beauty of the tree arise? Shape, size, color, touch, and the like are simply the names we call our sensations, and no amount of study of them can ever bring us to the notion of beauty in the tree. Beauty must therefore arise from some nonmaterial relation between the tree and myself. "I fancy," he told Arthur, "that there is Something right outside time and place, which did not create matter, as the Christians say, but is matter's great enemy: and that Beauty is the call of the spirit in that Something to the spirit in us." It was a long step upward for the atheist.

At this stage Lewis was more or less in the position of his character Mark in *That Hideous Strength*. The novel describes how Mark, who had grown up an unbeliever and materialist, was subjected to torture in an effort to get him to "believe" in a materialism more perverse than he had ever dreamed of. Under these circumstances "the idea of the Straight or Normal . . . grew stronger and more solid in his mind." Finally, it was like "a kind of mountain." Mark "had never before known what an Idea meant: he had always thought till now that they were things inside one's own head." But under persecution he came to understand that an idea is "something which obviously existed quite independently of himself and had hard rock surfaces which would not give, surfaces he could cling to."

Lewis himself was now discovering that things like beauty and the Straight have unexpected roots. Later on, debating with his friend Owen Barfield, he would be forced to the conviction that logic involves "participation in a cosmic *Logos*." At the time of this exchange with Greeves he still meant by "spiritual" something more nearly from nature upwards than from heaven downwards. But it is clear enough that substantial straws were blowing in the wind of Lewis's atheism.

Another deep-seated belief of this period, which Lewis was later to repudiate, was that of general or universal evolution. For some time he had worked on the lengthy narrative poem *Dymer*. The main idea, he wrote Arthur, was that of "develop-ment by self-destruction; . . . nature produces man only to conquer her, and man produces a future or higher generation to conquer the ideals of the last." This is a Keatsian idea, and Lewis was later to speak against it often. Yet it is significant that he adds of *Dymer*: "The background proceeds on the old assumption of good *outside* and *opposed to* the cosmic order." That is, somewhere outside the cosmos there appears to be a Good.

After the war Lewis returned to Oxford to complete his education, earning many honors along the way. As he commenced his college work anew he ran into a whole nest of men who were both Christians and intellectuals. He came to notice a wide gap between mere morality and "holiness" — his own word — in men like Nevill Coghill, J. R. R. Tolkien, A. K. Hamilton Jenkin, and, particularly, Owen Barfield. More and more he turned to the reading of distinctively religious writers. He read Jakob Boehme and, though not fully able to understand him, felt that he was talking of "something tremendously real." It was for Lewis another experience like *Phantastes*, "not like a book at all, but like a thunderclap. Heaven defend us — what things there are knocking about the world!" So compelling was the reading of Boehme that he attributed the effect to some local circumstance — perhaps the weather — and determined to try reading him again later.

The stream of God's calling in Lewis's life had already made many turns and tumbled over many rapids. Now it began to run deeper. He reexamined the quality of much of his lifelong reading and concluded that writers like Gibbon, Voltaire, Mill, Shaw, and Wells, who were well suited to his anti-Christian views, were thin and shallow, while writers whom he had most admired had a quality that suggested Christianity. George Herbert in particular he found superlative in conveying "the very quality of life as we actually live it from moment to moment; but the wretched fellow, instead of doing it all directly, insisted on mediating it through what I would still have called 'the Christian mythology.'"

All the while Lewis was maturing as a literary critic, and the insight into what makes a writer great became at the same time an insight into holiness. He was also continuing to review his philosophical outlook. Earlier he had experienced Lucretius, occultism, spiritualism, magic, theosophy, and pantheism in various forms. When logical positivism came onto the scene, Lewis equated it with the "ruthless dialectic" of his old tutor Kirkpatrick. Looking back, Lewis first felt that it was God himself who had kept him from getting too deeply involved in any of these movements. Perhaps it was the tremendous joy produced in him by reading such authors as George MacDonald and G. K. Chesterton which enabled him to survive the New Psychology that swept through Oxford and overwhelmed him for a time with the idea that his whole imaginative world, so large an element in his life, was no more than wishful thinking.

Reading Henri Bergson taught Lewis to "relish energy, fertility, and urgency; the resource, the triumphs, and even the insolence, of things that grow" and of "resonant, dogmatic, flaming, unanswerable people" like Beethoven, Titian, and Goethe. Also Bergson persuaded him to accept the universe and life as existent fact, "the nearest thing to a religious experience which I had had since my prep. school days."

Next he went through a period in which he tried to combine the conception on the one hand of a "real" universe with the belief on the other that subjective thought and moral judgment are legitimate avenues to truth. Barfield convinced him that such a mixture would not do and forced him to turn from realism to idealism, the conception "that the whole universe was, in the last resort, mental; that our logic was participation in a cosmic *Logos*."

Even though he then turned to Absolute Idealism, he still did not see how this pointed in the direction of Christianity. "I thought that 'the Christian myth' conveyed to unphilosophic minds as much of the truth, that is of Absolute Idealism, as they were capable of grasping. . . . Those who could not rise to the notion of the Absolute would come nearer the truth by belief in 'a God' than by disbelief. Those who could not understand how, as Reasoners, we participated in a timeless and therefore deathless world, would get a symbolic shadow of the truth by believing in a life after death." Lewis had always loved the idea of calling his soul his own, of not being interfered with. But logic itself — or rather Logic Himself — had begun to hem him in.

Now the last move or two began to take place. Lewis came upon Samuel Alexander's *Space, Time and Deity* and in reading it made a discovery that, as he says, "flashed a new light back on my whole life." In a word, he discovered that one cannot at the same instant hope and think about hoping. Hope and reflective thought about it can alternate rapidly, but they are two different things. All his life Lewis had been beset with a hope for something for which he could find no better word than Joy. Reading Alexander, he saw that his lifelong search for Joy had really been misdirected. His quest had been like that of the boy John, whom he was later to write about in *Pilgrim's Regress*. Turning away from the hateful Landlord to whom his parents had recommended him, John one day got a glimpse of a delicious Island and heard music so sweet as to set him searching for more of it. He went through a long series of unsatisfying and sometimes bruising experiences until he at last found the Joy he had sought in the Landlord whom he had so thoroughly misunderstood. On Alexander's terms John had been trying to re-create the experience of Joy inside himself when what he really wanted was not a sensation but a real Object.

Alexander made it clear to Lewis that the feeling of Joy he had been trying to capture was no more than a by-product, not the real thing. It was "merely the mental track left by the passage of Joy — not the wave but the wave's imprint on the sand." No image or sensation could ever be equal to the thing of which it was only the vestige. Images and sensations said, "I am only a reminder. Look! What do I remind you of?" The idea took shape that every desire is turned not to itself but to its object and owes its very character to its object. "It is the object that makes the desire itself desirable or hateful."

Suddenly Lewis saw that his lifelong search for Joy was different from what he had ever supposed. He found that "in deepest solitude there is a road right out of the self, a commerce with something which, by refusing to identify itself with any object of the senses, or anything whereof we have biological or social need, or anything imagined, or any state of our own minds, proclaims itself sheerly objective." He realized now that man has "a root in the Absolute, which is the utter reality." It was a discovery that most people never make; in Lewis it was like the blow of a sledge-hammer. The relentless and supposedly atheistic logic taught him by the Great Knock was strangely producing a sturdy plant ready almost for blossoms.

Alexander made Lewis see that the world is made up of real and abstractive experiences. A toothache is real, but thoughts about that toothache are abstract thoughts. An apple is real, but to multiply six apples times six apples is abstractive. Kissing one's sweetheart is a real experience, but analyzing that kiss is abstractive; and analysis is certain to dissipate the reality of a kiss. God is real, but to inquire into doctrines of God is abstractive. It is impossible to have the two experiences at the same moment. Both experiences have their value, but they should never be taken as equivalents. It is a predicament we carry from one end of life to the other. If we fail to understand the clear difference between the two, not only are we thinking badly but we may be missing the glowing delight and wonder of things natural and supernatural.

One day perched atop the bus going east from Magdalen College to his home, Lewis had the deeply quiet experience of decision. "I felt myself being, there and then, given a free choice. I could open the door or keep it shut. . . . Neither choice was presented as a duty; no threat or promise was attached to either, though I knew that to open the door or take off the corslet meant the incalculable." Heaven's hound now had Lewis in sight. To use his own words: "Amiable agnostics will talk cheerfully about 'man's search for God.' To me, as I then was, they might as well have talked about the mouse's search for the cat." In Christian terms, the Spirit of God now had him securely but lovingly in hand.

As his antagonism to Christianity diminished Lewis naturally faced the complexities of Christian doctrine. He puzzled over how Christ's death on the cross "saved" a man. He saw clearly enough that there were two directions — one motivating a person towards Christ, the other propelling him to hell so that nothing short of a miracle could save him. "What I couldn't see was how the life and death of Someone Else (whoever he was) 2000 years ago could help us here and now — except in so far as his *example* helped us." But, significant as example was, Lewis came to understand that following it was not fundamentally Christianity. He read the New Testament and found there "something quite different and very mysterious, expressed in those phrases I had so often ridiculed ('propitiation' — 'sacrifice' — 'the blood of the Lamb'), expressions which I could only interpret in senses that seemed to me either silly or shocking."

In this dilemma, friends at Oxford, including J. R. R. Tolkien, helped him see the difference between the mere doctrine or expository statement of the incarnation, crucifixion, and resurrection of Christ and the living actuality, an actuality that goes deeper than language. That is, Christ Himself is larger than any possible doctrinal statement about Him can ever be. It was more of what Alexander had taught him.

Lewis became on occasion Greeves's teacher in spiritual things. To the argument of one of Arthur's friends that the Gospels do not teach the atonement, that the evangelists would have so taught had they the slightest excuse, and hence that Christ did not teach this doctrine, Lewis replied that the Epistles were written before the Gospels and that the apostles did therefore teach the atonement just following the crucifixion. Furthermore, he said, to remove the idea of sacrifice from Christianity would be to eliminate significance from both Judaism and paganism, since both point toward Christ. "Can one believe there was just *nothing* in that persistent *motif* of blood, death, and resurrection, which runs like a black and scarlet cord through all the greater myths — through Balder and Dionysus and

Adonis and the Grail too? Surely the history of the human mind hangs together better if you suppose that all this was the first shadowy approach of something whose reality came with Christ — even if we can't at present fully understand that something." It was a subject on which Lewis was to write at length as the years passed.

Arthur inquired of his friend about the notion of a good God and an evil world. That Arthur thought this question would be "elementary" for Lewis evidences the progress Arthur had noticed in his friend. Lewis disagreed. It was not elementary for him, and it might not be so even for the angels. Supposing that Arthur had in mind not the logical problem of how God might produce a world containing evil but the practical issue of God's particular concern with man's evil, Lewis proceeded. Arthur had spoken of God as having in Himself, at least potentially, the opposites of good and evil. This Lewis denied, citing the idea from the medieval definition of God as "that which has no opposite." God, he declared, must be regarded as the ultimate beyond the great opposites, "just as space is neither bigness or smallness but that in which the distinctions of big and small arise." Evil may thus be "included" under God, even though the Scriptures make clear that in Him is no darkness at all.

Arthur had remarked that there is no good without evil; Lewis insisted that it might be just the opposite — no evil without good. He clarified this by the illustration of a person walking a dog. If the animal gets his lead wrapped around a post and tries to continue running forward, he will only tighten the lead the more. Both dog and owner are after the same end, forward motion, but the owner must resist the dog by pulling him opposite. The master, sharing the same intention but understanding better than the dog where he wants really to go, takes an action precisely opposite to that of the dog's will. We might say it is in this sense that God "includes" evil.

Similarly God understands and shares the right wish that is at the root of our evil — the desire for forward movement toward ultimate happiness — and the sinful post around which we have

tangled our leads. But by the fact of His sovereign knowledge of what is actually good for us, He must *not* sympathize or agree with us, but the opposite. In later years Lewis taught over and over that "Aslan is not a tame lion," that is, Christ is loving but He is not at all weak. He will not indulge us. On the contrary, His very nature makes him unyielding to anything other than our absolute need of Himself.

Lewis concluded that a God of everlasting love and grace can only wish for the eternal happiness of every man. He wants precisely what any man, apart from his evil will, really wants. "Only because he has laid up *real* goods for us to desire are we able to go wrong by snatching at them in greedy, misdirected ways. The truth is that evil is not a real *thing* at all, like good. It is simply good *spoiled*." Evil is a parasite on good. Lewis ends his argument by citing George MacDonald's remark, "Only God understands evil and hates it." If only we could see with God's eyes, rather than our fallen ones, we should always go His way.

But in spite of such clear thinking the young university don preferred his freedom, or what he thought to be his freedom, to any acceptance of Christianity. But he was beginning to feel God bearing down on him. Unable to go on with his ordinary duties, he put them aside. During the Trinity Term in 1929 he knelt down, prayed, and confessed that God really is God. In due course he and his brother left on a sunny morning by motorcycle for Whipsnade zoo. "When we set out," said Lewis, "I did not believe that Jesus Christ is the Son of God, and when we reached the zoo I did." The long journey into Light had finished and also had begun.

Even before he had fully accepted Christ as his Savior, he had set out to seek the total implications of his faith. In so doing he felt he must take a tenacious look at the real roots of sin in his life. He wrote Arthur, "I seem to have been supported in respect to chastity and anger more continually, and with less struggle, for the last ten days." He discovered "ludicrous and terrible things" about himself, the worst being a great depth of pride. When he had looked at his sins one by one, and painfully confessed them, pride arose and congratulated him on how well he had done. It was a state of mind he was to wrestle with personally and write about for the rest of his life.

But along with humiliation came at times great joy. He went through the experience of finding skies bluer and grass greener. "Today," he wrote Arthur, "I got such a sudden intense feeling of delight that it sort of stopped me in my walk and spun me round. Indeed the sweetness was so great, and seemed so to affect the whole body as well as the mind, that it gave me pause." And later, "Everything seems . . . to be beginning again and one has the sense of immortality." And again, "I really seem to have had youth given back to me lately."

Yet for the most part these were times of self-analysis before God. A close look at the devious ego differed little from a look at the devil himself. Once he had joked at the idea of Satan and hell; now he came to a deep conviction of their reality. At the same time his conception of heaven was growing more real. He concluded that man's lifelong yearning is actually for Joy and that all earthly joys are faint shadows of the great Joy arising from the total confession of Jesus Christ as the lodestone of one's heart.

He remained aware that progress in the practice of Christianity is both necessary and difficult. "I am appalled," he wrote Arthur, "to see how much of the change I thought I had undergone lately was only imaginary. The real work seems still to be done." He went back through his life to remember and re-evaluate his relationships with people. He discovered that even the act of writing required the valley of humiliation. In response to Arthur's discouragement over his efforts to publish, Lewis warned that the yen to publish is spiritually dangerous. "One must reach the point of 'not caring two straws about his own status' before he can wish wholly for God's kingdom, not his own, to be established." Death to ambition as such will be the beginning of new life. Above all, the part of a man which puts success first must be humiliated if a man is ever to be really free.

Lewis understood that in his writing, as in everything else, mere ambition was to be renounced in favor of the will of God.

Perhaps here we have an explanation of the power of his books in the lives of millions of people. "It is not your business to succeed," he wrote Arthur, "but to do right: when you have done so, the rest lies with God." That was henceforth to be his attitude as a writer, as a teacher, as the member of a household, and in his private life.

As early as the age of six Lewis had felt *Sehnsucht,* a longing for he knew not what. The most poignant experience of it had been one summer day when he was standing beside a currant bush. The little boy had felt suddenly arise in him "as if from a depth not of years but of centuries" a longing so deep that, as he described it later, "in a certain sense everything else that had ever happened to me was insignificant by comparison." He sought hard to satisfy that longing, and he found every experience but one to be counterfeit. That one was God. Like John in *The Pilgrim's Regress,* Lewis fairly well had to be dragged into the Kingdom, but when he arrived there he knew with a great knowing what precisely the source of his longing had been.

For at least twenty-three years God patiently let His light fall on the child, the boy, the young atheist, the sinner, until finally in his rooms at Magdalen he acknowledged that God was God. Thereafter, like St. Paul, Lewis grew to hate many of the things he had once loved and to love some he had hated. The conception of Jesus, Yeshua, as a man-created myth was dropped. Gone, too, was the sophistication that had once assured Arthur that "educated and thinking people" reject the idea of Christ as Savior. These ideas were not only abandoned, they were reversed; and Lewis became their brilliant opponent.

All along he had clung to the strong belief that he was his own free agent. Now he discovered that such freedom was not actually freedom, and that true freedom arose from bondslavery to Jesus Christ. It was all very Pauline!

Images
of His World

OXFORD. Though historical fact and legend are intertwined in accounts of its origins, Oxford University probably began in the late 1160s, when English scholars were expelled by the nationalistic French from the University of Paris. In the beginning, Oxford's Masters lectured in Latin. There were no buildings or endowments, and the pupils paid fees for the lectures they attended. Many of the medieval traditions remain a feature of life at Oxford. Undergraduates still wear academic gowns to lectures, conferences with tutors, chapel, and dinners in the residence halls.

The university is a federation of its colleges. Its main functions are sponsoring lectures, supervising examinations, and conferring degrees. There are thirty-one colleges at Oxford — the oldest, University College, dating from 1249, the newest, St. Catherine's, from 1962. Five of the colleges are for women, and one is coeducational. An undergraduate is accepted for admission by a particular college, and his work there is individually supervised by a tutor. In addition to attending lectures given by the university, the student confers once or twice a week with his tutor to discuss a paper he has prepared.

The college buildings, arranged around a quadrangle and connected by cloisters, are the residences of the students and tutors. Adjacent to them are gardens and athletic fields.

C. S. Lewis's first glimpse of Oxford was late in 1916 when he came there to sit for a scholarship. When he began his study at the university, he wrote Arthur Greeves that the place was "absolutely ripping." He was particularly fond of his own college, University, and wrote his father about wandering over it one evening "into all sorts of parts where I had never been before, where mullioned windows are dark with ivy that no one has bothered to cut since the war emptied the rooms they belong to."

A typical day in his life began about seven o'clock, when he arose. As Lewis describes it, he read for an hour and a half. "I then went down to the bathroom and had first a hot and a cold bath — which is 'done' here. We are gradually getting to know people and a very senior man, Butler, had asked us to 'brekker' [breakfast] this morning. I arrived in his rooms a little too early, and thus had an opportunity of studying his books, which I always consider the best introduction to a new acquaintance. I was pleased to find Keats, Shelley, Oscar Wilde, Dante and Villon, as well as Plutarch and one of the lately executed Sinn Fein poets. . . . I was just trying to find out the publisher of the nice Plutarch, when Butler arrived with the other guests, Edgell and a certain Edwards, and we sat down to brekker. I like Butler exceedingly . . . it seems that he knows Yeats quite well, and also Gilbert Murray. . . . After brekker we all decided that a bathe would be a very sound plan." They rode on their bicycles through Oxford and down to the river while Sunday morning church bells pealed and spires glittered in the sun.

Oxford, High Street

Looking east along High Street

Magdalen College: a cloister and the chapel

One of Lewis's joys during the nearly thirty years he spent as a Fellow and Tutor at Magdalen College was the beauty of his external surroundings. "My big sitting room looks north and from it I see nothing, not even a gable or a spire, to remind me that I am in a town. I look down on a stretch of level grass which passes into a grove of immemorial forest trees, at present coloured autumn red. Over this stray the deer. They are erratic in their habits. Some mornings when I look out there will be half a dozen chewing the cud just underneath me, and on others there will be none in sight — or one little stag (not much bigger than a calf and looking too slender for the weight of his antlers) standing still and sending through the fog that queer little bark which is these beasts' 'moo'. It is a sound that will soon be as familiar to me as the cough of the cows in the field at home, for I hear it day and night."

"My smaller sitting room and bedroom look out southwards across a broad lawn to the main buildings of Magdalen with the tower beyond it."

Lewis's rooms at Magdalen were on the second floor near the center.

Often Lewis would walk this path, known as Addison's Walk because Joseph Addison had been fond of it during his days at Oxford two centuries earlier. His good friend Nevill Coghill recalls meeting Lewis there one day, "his round, rubicund face beaming with pleasure to itself. When we came within speaking distance, I said, 'Hullo, Jack! You look very pleased with yourself; what is it?' 'I believe,' he answered, with a modest smile of triumph, 'I *believe* I have proved that the Renaissance never happened in England. *Alternatively,*' he held up his hand to prevent my astonished exclamation, 'that if it did, *it had no importance!*'"

Magdalen Tower across Angel and Greyhound Meadow, along the Cherwell River

"I usually go and bathe before breakfast now at a very little place up the Cherwell called 'Parson's Pleasure.' I always swim (on chest) down to a bend straight towards the sun, see some hills in the distance across the water, then turn and come again to land going on my back and looking up at the willow trees above me."

The River Cherwell

"Conversation Piece," by Alan Sorrell, 1954. Sitting in the Magdalen Senior Common Room are Fellows (clockwise from the left front) Alan Raitt, Colin Hardie, A. W. Adams, Gilbert Ryle, T. S. R. Boase, Godfrey Driver, C. S. Lewis, James Griffiths, and J. A. W. Bennett.

"As you come out of our college gate you see All Souls and just beyond it the grey spire of St. Mary's Church. You know what real Gothic is like: all little pinnacles with every kind of ornament on them and in the snow they look like a wintry forest hung up against the dark sky, and always associated in one's mind with the sound of bells."

St. Mary the Virgin's, the University church, dates from the thirteenth and fifteenth centuries. In the 1830s John Henry Cardinal Newman preached there; a century later Lewis addressed overflow crowds in the church on several occasions. In 1939 and 1941, his well-known sermons "Learning in War-time" and "The Weight of Glory" were delivered in St. Mary's.

St. Mary the Virgin's

Oxford is, Lewis said, a "dangerous place for a book lover. Every second shop has something you want." According to Warren Lewis, his brother soon learned to discipline such inclinations: "In his younger days he was something of a bibliophile, but in middle and later life he very seldom bought a book if he could consult it in the Bodleian: long years of poverty, self-inflicted but grinding, had made this economical habit second nature to him — a fact that contributed, no doubt, to the extra-ordinarily retentive character of his memory."

Broad Street, showing part of the Bodleian Library (right)

In March 1928 Lewis wrote to his father, "I spend all my mornings in the Bodleian. . . . If only one could smoke and if only there were upholstered chairs, this would be one of the most delightful places in the world. I sit in 'Duke Humphrey's Library', the oldest part, a fifteenth-century building with a very beautiful wooden painted ceiling above me and a little mullioned window on my left hand through which I look down on the garden of Exeter, where this morning I see the sudden squalls of wind and rain driving the first blossoms off the fruit trees and snowing the lawn with them. At the bottom of the room the gilt bust of Charles I, presented by Laud, faces the gilt bust of Strafford—poor Strafford. The library itself—I mean the books — is mostly in a labyrinth of cellars under the neighbouring squares. This room however is full of books which stand in little cases at right angles to the wall, so that between each pair there is a kind of little 'box' — in the public-house sense of the word — and in these boxes one sits and reads."

Radcliffe Camera, part of the Bodleian Library

The Bodleian Tower

Statue of the Earl of Pembroke, a courtier at Queen Elizabeth I's court. Among other activities of his was his encouragement of the colonization of America. Pembroke College at Oxford was named for him.

For more than forty years Lewis's closest friend was Owen Barfield, a solicitor, who was also interested, from a philosophical angle, in the history of human consciousness. Lewis called Barfield the type of everyone's "Second Friend . . . the man who disagrees with you about everything. He is not so much the *alter ego* as the antiself. Of course he shares your interests; otherwise he would not become your friend at all. But he has approached them all at a different angle. He has read all the right books but has got the wrong thing out of every one. It is as if he spoke your language but mispronounced it. How can he be so nearly right and yet, invariably, just not right? He is as fascinating (and infuriating) as a woman. When you set out to correct his heresies, you find that he forsooth has decided to correct yours. And then you go at it, hammer and tongs, far into the night, night after night, or walking through fine country that neither gives a glance to, each learning the weight of the other's punches, and often more like mutually respectful enemies than friends. Actually (though it never seems so at the time) you modify one another's thought; out of this perpetual dogfight a community of mind and a deep affection emerge. But I think he changed me a good deal more than I him."

Here we see a gentleman (not identified) engaged on seeing whether a departure from dry academical methods and a newer, freer theory of knowledge may not get some new images out of the mirror The mirror seems to be playing up well so far. Meanwhile the clouds have ebbed to his ankles. Something like despairing hands stretches to reach from behind but he doesn't notice them. Overhead I detect a curious figuration of cloud that fancy may interpret as a gigantic face in laughter. The hammer and chisel are occult science, yoga, "meditation" (in technical sense) etc.

An orful example. Study of a gentleman reaching vainly for the inner reality he has scorned, while he shrinks in horror from the phantom he has created on the black wall from which he has succeeding in chipping off all the looking-glass. (Only those who are not poets cd. get as far as this, of course) On a second mirror invisible to him but visible to his neighbours, ambulance, asylum, cemetery appears successively.

"The Great War" was the name Lewis and Barfield gave to the philosophical exchanges between them. "It was never, thank God, a quarrel, though it could have become one in a moment if he had used to me anything like the violence I allowed myself to him. But it was an almost incessant disputation, sometimes by letter and sometimes face to face, which lasted for years. And this Great War was one of the turning points of my life." These drawings and accompanying commentary reveal the banter that sometimes offset the serious discussions of the "Great War."

Nevill Coghill, now retired, was Merton Professor of English Literature at Oxford and Fellow and Tutor in English Literature at Exeter College. One of his best-known pupils was Richard Burton. Lewis met Coghill in a discussion class at Oxford in 1922. About him Lewis said, "The very first words he spoke marked him out from the ten or twelve others who were present, a man after my own heart. . . . I soon had the shock of discovering that he — clearly the most intelligent and best-informed man in the class — was a Christian and a thorough-going supernaturalist." As undergraduates, Coghill writes, the two of them "would stride over Hinksey and Cumnor — we walked almost as fast as we talked — disputing and quoting, as we looked for the dark dingles and the tree-topped hills of Matthew Arnold. . . . Lewis, with the gusto of a Chesterton or a Belloc, would suddenly roar out a passage of poetry that he had newly discovered and memorized, particularly if it were in Old English, a language novel and enchanting to us both for its heroic attitudes and crashing rhythms."

Hinksey Hill

At Coghill's urging Lewis borrowed his copy of *The Place of the Lion* by Charles Williams, an editor with Oxford University Press in London. "Twenty-four hours later I found myself, for the first time in my life, writing to an author I had never met to congratulate him on his book. By return of post I had an answer from Williams, who had received my letter when he was on the point of writing a similar letter to me about my *Allegory of Love*. After this . . . we soon met and our friendship rapidly grew inwardly to the bone. Until 1939 that friendship had to subsist on occasional meetings, though, even thus, he had already become as dear to all my Oxford friends as he was to me. . . . But in 1939 the Oxford University Press, and he with it, was evacuated to Oxford." When Williams died in 1945 Lewis wrote to a friend, "I have also become much acquainted with grief now through the death of my great friend Charles Williams, my friend of friends, the comforter of all our little set, the most angelic man. The odd thing is that his death has made my faith stronger than it was a week ago. And I find that all that talk about 'feeling that he is closer to us than before' isn't just talk. It's just what it does feel like — and I can't put it into words."

The Inklings was a group of kindred spirits who met weekly in Lewis's rooms at Magdalen, "theoretically to talk about literature, but in fact nearly always to talk about something better. What I owe to them all is incalculable. . . . Is any pleasure on earth as great as a circle of Christian friends by a good fire?" Some of the Inklings over the years were Warren H. Lewis, Owen Barfield, J. R. R. Tolkien, Nevill Coghill, Charles Williams, Gervase Mathew, Colin Hardie, Hugo Dyson, Dr. Robert Havard, Canon Adam Fox, and Commander Dundas-Grant. Warren Lewis describes the ritual of an Inklings meeting: "When half a dozen or so had arrived, tea would be produced, and then when pipes were well alight Jack would say, 'Well, has nobody got anything to read to us?' Out would come a manuscript, and we would settle down to sit in judgement upon it — real unbiased judgement, too, since we were no mutual admiration society: praise for good work was unstinted, but censure for bad work — or even not-so-good work — was often brutally frank. . . . Sometimes, though not often, it would happen that no one had anything to read us. On these occasions the fun would be riotous, with Jack at the top of his form and enjoying every minute . . . an outpouring of wit, nonsense, whimsy, dialectical swordplay, and pungent judgement such as I have rarely heard equalled. . . . And there was also another ritual gathering, subsidiary to the Inklings proper: the same company used to meet for an hour or so before lunch every Tuesday at the Eagle and Child [a pub] in St. Giles', better known as the Bird and Baby."

Gervase Mathew, a member of the Dominican Order since 1928, was University Lecturer in Byzantine Studies from 1941 to 1971. During his career he participated in a number of archaeological and anthropological expeditions to Africa and Arabia. He met with the Inklings, and contributed an essay on marriage and courtly love in fourteenth-century England to the collection of essays Lewis edited in honor of Charles Williams.

About his colleague H. V. D. Dyson, Lecturer and Tutor at the University of Reading, later Fellow of Merton College and Tutor in English Literature, Lewis wrote, "He is a most fastidious bookman . . . but as far from being a dilettante as anyone can be; a burly man, both in mind and body, with the stamp of the war on him, which begins to be a pleasing rarity, at any rate in civilian life. Lest anything should be lacking, he is a Christian and a lover of cats."

J. R. R. Tolkien, Emeritus Professor of English Language and Literature at Merton College, Oxford. Although a specialist in Anglo-Saxon and Middle English, he is better known as the author of *The Hobbit* and *The Lord of the Rings,* stories about hobbits, elves, ents, orcs, and fabulous adventure. Lewis was instrumental in persuading Tolkien to bring out a portion of the epic-like story on which he had worked most of his life. When the first volume of *The Lord of the Rings* appeared, Lewis said of it, "This book is lightning from a clear sky. . . . Not content to create his own story, he creates, with an almost insolent prodigality, the whole world in which it is to move, with its own theology, myths, geography, history, palaeography, languages, and orders of being."

"When I began teaching for the English Faculty, I made two other friends, both Christians (those queer people seemed to pop up on every side) who were later to give me much help in getting over the last stile. They were H. V. D. Dyson (then of Reading) and J. R. R. Tolkien. Friendship with the latter marked the breakdown of two old prejudices. At my first coming into the world I had been (implicitly) warned never to trust a Papist, and at my first coming into the English Faculty (explicitly) never to trust a philologist. Tolkien was both."

Colin Hardie, Fellow of Magdalen College and Tutor in Classics. One evening as Lewis, Hardie, and some others were together, "someone started the question 'whether God can understand His own necessity'; whereupon Hardie got down St. Thomas's *Summa* and after ferreting in the index pronounced, without any intention of being funny, 'He doesn't understand anything.' This led to great amusement, the best being an imaginary scene of God trying to explain the theory of vicarious punishment to Socrates."

Lord David Cecil, Goldsmiths' Professor of English Literature at Oxford until his retirement in 1970, and the distinguished author of many books, shared with Lewis a keen interest in Jane Austen's novels. Lord David regarded Lewis as the really great man at Oxford.

Lewis's publisher Jocelyn Gibb was a close friend. After Lewis's death, he wrote: "It was our privilege to be the publishers of his religious and children's books for thirty years. To know him, to enjoy his friendship, was a wonderful, if sometimes testing, experience. It was not that he expected perfection, for he was essentially a kind, tolerant man, but he derived such pleasure in seeing the striving for perfection that one often felt on one's mettle. Lewis, however, was not an exacting person. To engage in a conversation with him was stimulating and at the same time comforting. He always brought out the best in people so that you felt you were making as much a contribution as he was to the parry of words. That was the way. And woe betide you if you made a woolly remark or betrayed an obvious weakness in your argument. He would be on you like a flash; not unkind or rough, but questioning, making you explain your reasons — if you had any. . . . He had a well-developed, spontaneous sense of the ridiculous. . . . He was at home talking to all sorts of people. . . . Some of his dearest friends were non-scholars who had something to contribute to that clear, imaginative mind of his."

Lewis often took the #2 bus from Magdalen College to his home in Headington Quarry. Although the college stipend included rooms and meals, it was usual for a tutor with family responsibilities to "live out" with his family.

THE KILNS. From 1930 until his death in 1963, home for Lewis was in Headington Quarry, a suburb of Oxford, at The Kilns, so-called because the furnaces for brick-making were at that time still in place behind the house. Shortly after moving there, Lewis wrote to Greeves, "There is one odd thing I have been noticing since we came to our new house, which is much more in the country, and it is this. Hitherto there has always been something not so much in the landscape as in every single visual impression (say a cloud, a robin, or a ditch) in Ireland, which I lacked in England: something for which homeliness is an inadequate word. This something I find I am now getting in England — the feeling of connectedness, of being part of it. I suppose I have been growing into the soil here much more since the move." Lewis appreciated the house as well as its setting: "This house has a good night atmosphere about it: in the sense that I have never been in a place where one is less likely to get the creeps: a place less sinister. Good life must have been lived here before us. If it is haunted, it is haunted by good spirits, perhaps such things are the result of fantasy, yet the feelings are real."

In his early life Lewis rode a bicycle, but he never drove an automobile. When he wished to leave Magdalen for The Kilns, either someone would come for him or he would take the bus across the Cherwell and through Headington. He would walk the few blocks from the bus stop to his home. If he had time and the weather was good, Lewis would sometimes walk the entire way back to the college, savoring particularly the view of Oxford from the steep brow of Headington Hill. In recent years, new houses have been built around The Kilns and the little lane that once led from the street to the house has been replaced by a paved roadway. The new settlement is called Lewis Close.

When Lewis's army roommate Paddy Moore was killed in World War I, Lewis became, by an agreement the two of them had made, a "foster son" to Paddy's widowed mother, Mrs. Jane King Moore, and a "foster brother" to her young daughter Maureen. Recently Maureen Moore Blake was designated Lady Dunbar of Hempriggs and acquired a castle in Scotland. After borrowing a copy of George MacDonald's "The Princess and the Goblin" from Maureen, Lewis wrote, "This child has a well-stocked library of fairy tales which form her continual reading — an excellent taste at her age, I think, which will lead her in later life to romance and poetry and not to the twaddling novels that make up the diet of most educated women apparently."

"The other blessing [of my childhood] was my brother. Though three years my senior, he never seemed to be an elder brother; we were allies, not to say confederates, from the first. Yet we were very different." After Major W. H. Lewis's retirement from the army he came to make his home with his beloved brother. At The Kilns he wrote several books on seventeenth-century French history and acted as secretary to his brother in handling the increasing volume of correspondence addressed to Lewis. At his death in April 1973 Major Lewis was living at The Kilns.

"Much of Lewis's life was hidden from me," Nevill Coghill wrote. "He almost never spoke about himself, in my hearing at least: though once, shortly after his marriage, when he brought his wife to lunch with me, he said to me, looking at her across the grassy quadrangle, 'I never expected to have, in my sixties, the happiness that passed me by in my twenties.' " In large part Joy Davidman, who had corresponded with Lewis for a long time, turned to Christianity through reading his writings. She said that both she and her first husband William Gresham had been active in the American Communist Party and had grown

Joy Davidman Lewis and C. S. Lewis in 1958, outside The Kilns. Both were in poor health at the time of this photograph.

Lewis in his study at The Kilns in 1963

up in a generation which "sucked in atheism with its canned milk." In April 1956 she and Lewis were married in a civil ceremony; a year later they had an ecclesiastical ceremony, after which Joy came to live at The Kilns. She was known to be suffering from cancer of the thigh, and in April 1957 Lewis wrote that she was "bed-ridden and dying. . . . I lead the life of a hospital orderly." But there was a remission, and a couple of months later they had a belated honeymoon. In October 1959 the cancer reappeared. The couple traveled to Greece, fulfilling Joy's longtime wish, and not long after their return she died. The poem on the memorial tablet at the crematorium near The Kilns was written by Lewis.

Douglas Gresham

As small boys, Douglas and David Gresham became Lewis's stepsons. David has recently been graduated from Cambridge University, and Douglas is now a businessman in Australia.

David Gresham

F. W. Paxford was Lewis's gardener for thirty-four years — "our indispensable factotum," Lewis called him. With his efficient help Lewis and Mrs. Moore planted an orchard on one side of the property, raised rabbits and chickens (for which it was Lewis's longtime task to spade worms), set out flowers, particularly a rose arbor, leveled the lawn in front of the house, and planted a vegetable patch. According to Walter Hooper, one of the major characters in *The Silver Chair*, Puddleglum the marsh-wiggle, is modeled after Paxford, "an inwardly optimistic, outwardly pessimistic, dear, frustrating, shrewd countryman of immense integrity."

Inside The Kilns: upper left, the bedroom in which Lewis died; lower left, the living room, formerly Lewis's study; above, a handmade wardrobe that has been in the Lewis family for several generations

Molly and Len Miller. Molly was Lewis's housekeeper for many years. When Len retired, both came to live at The Kilns and care for Major Lewis until his death.

Beyond the lawn of The Kilns and at the bottom of the hill was a pond where clay had once been removed for brickmaking. Swimming in this pond, either alone or with friends like Tolkien, was one of Lewis's chief pleasures. "I know the pond looks dirty, but as a matter of fact one comes out perfectly clean. I wish you could join me as I board the punt in the before-breakfast solitude and push out from under the dark shadow of trees onto the full glare of the open water, usually sending the moor hens and their chicks scudding away into the reeds, half flying and half swimming with a delicious flurry of silver drops. Then I tie up to the projecting stump in the middle and dive off the stern of the punt."

70

"Any patch of sunlight in a wood will show you something about the sun which you could never get from reading books on astronomy. These pure and spontaneous pleasures are 'patches of Godlight' in the woods of our experience."

Two of the pubs near Oxford which Lewis often frequented were The Trout (right) and The Six Bells. Some of Lewis's American readers had written him to inquire about his views on drinking alcoholic beverages. His response to them was in no uncertain terms: "I have always in my books been concerned simply to put forward 'mere' Christianity, and am no guide on these (most regrettable) 'inter-denominational' questions. I do however strongly object to the tyrannic and unscriptural insolence of anything that calls itself a Church and makes teetotalism a condition of membership. Apart from the more serious objection (that Our Lord Himself turned water into wine and made wine the medium of the only rite He imposed on all His followers), it is so provincial (what I believe you people call 'small town'). Don't they realize that Christianity arose in the Mediterranean world where, then as now, wine was as much part of the normal diet as bread?"

At the close of *Out of the Silent Planet* Ransom, having made the return trip from Mars in the increasingly stale atmosphere of the spaceship, finally landed back on the earth. "He stood in pitch-black night under torrential rain. With every pore of his body he drank it in: with every desire of his heart he embraced the smell of the field about him — a patch of his native planet where grass grew, where cows moved, where presently he would come to hedges and a gate. He had walked about half an hour when a vivid light behind him and a strong, momentary wind informed him that the space ship was no more. He felt very little interest. He had seen dim lights, the lights of men, ahead. A lighted door was open. There were voices from within and they were speaking English. There was a familiar smell. He pushed his way in, regardless of the surprise he was creating, and walked to the bar. 'A pint of bitter, please,' said Ransom."

Southwest of Oxford, near Cumnor

In an early letter to Greeves, Lewis explained the term "soaking machine" as a place to sit idly or sleepily doing nothing, in other words, a comfortable seat. Such places are, he suggested, "very scarce in England, owing to the strict customs which prevent the mildest trespassing. My new place is at the foot of a great oak, a few yards off a lane, and hidden therefrom by a little row of shrubs and small trees. Completely private, safe from sun, wind or rain, and on the ridge of the only rising ground (you couldn't call it a hill) about here, there with a notebook and pencil I can be free to write, etc., as at home."

Lewis enjoyed walking in this area. After a visit from Greeves in 1930 he wrote him, "on the day you left I went our usual walk through Old Headington, past that little isolated house which you admired, the brook, and then over two fields to our soaking machine. . . . I felt that sort of melancholy — you probably know it — which comes from walking through the same scenes through which you walked with a friend a few hours ago, when he has gone. . . . Mixed with this melancholy, however, . . . there was a freshness of solitude which itself on such occasions feels like a friend revisited."

"I've been wondering why these days of rain and wind in the summer have such a charm for me. Is it some offshoot of my general love of winter, and these days please me as a general foretaste of winter? As if the wind shook summer, and he buttoned his coat and said, 'Dear me, I'm beginning to get old.' Or is it that such days fall outside of the categories of one's conventional categories of the seasons, neither being typical summer days nor autumn days not typical anything, and therefore thwarting one's derivative reactions in all that has been already stereotyped in literature and painting. They force me to wake up and see the thing as it really is."

"A. K. Hamilton Jenkin . . . continued (what Arthur had begun) my education as a seeing, listening, smelling, receptive creature. Arthur had had his preference for the Homely. But Jenkin seemed to be able to enjoy everything; even ugliness. I learned from him that we should attempt a total surrender to whatever atmosphere was offering itself at the moment; in a squalid town to seek out those very places where its squalor rose to grimness and almost grandeur, on a dismal day to find the most dismal and dripping wood, on a windy day to seek the windiest ridge. There was no Betjemannic irony about it; only a serious, yet gleeful, determination to rub one's nose in the very quiddity of each thing, to rejoice in its being (so magnificently) what it was."

CAMBRIDGE. After long service at Oxford, Lewis was elected in 1954 to the Chair of Medieval and Renaissance English at Magdalene College, Cambridge, where he was to spend the last eight years of his life. In his inaugural lecture, *De Descriptione Temporum,* he endeavored to identify the greatest change in Western history, which he took to be the "birth of the machines" early in the nineteenth century.

As a University Lecturer, Lewis was no longer required to do tutorial work. Shortly before leaving Oxford, he wrote of his new position that "it means rather less work for rather more pay. I think I shall like Magdalene better than Magdalen. It's a tiny college (a perfect cameo architecturally) and they're all so old fashioned, and pious, and gentle and conservative — unlike this leftist, atheist, cynical, hard-boiled, huge Magdalen. Perhaps from being the fogey and 'old woman' here I shall become the *enfant terrible* there. It is nice to be still under the care of St. Mary Magdalene: she must by now understand my constitution better than a stranger would, don't you think?"

During his tenure at Cambridge Lewis generally returned to The Kilns each week. Often he traveled by train, a means of transportation disdained by some who found it too slow. Lewis wrote, "I find myself perfectly content in a slow train that crawls through green fields stopping at every station. . . . I get through a lot of reading and sometimes say my prayers."

As at Oxford, the beginnings of Cambridge were largely ecclesiastical and scholastic. The university took its rise in the twelfth century, as many of its medieval structures suggest. The first college to be established was Peterhouse, in 1284. Magdalene was founded in 1542, though some of its buildings are older.

Cambridge

Magdalene College from across the Cam River

80

The arched windows to the right were Lewis's.

Main entrance, Magdalene College

During his later years in Cambridge, when his health was poor, Lewis confined his beloved walking excursions to the nearby banks of the Cam River, which flows alongside Magdalene College.

The Fellows' Garden, Magdalene

Built in the late fifteenth century, the Magdalene Chapel has undergone many changes. Here, according to Professor R. W. Ladborough, late director of the Pepys Library at Magdalene, was the center of Lewis's life at Cambridge: "He attended weekday matins at eight o'clock, and when he was well enough, he walked in the Fellows' Garden beforehand."

J. A. W. Bennett, a pupil of Lewis at Oxford and his successor as Professor of Medieval and Renaissance English at Magdalene, said of him: "The whole man was in all his judgements and activities, and a discriminating zest for life, for 'common life', informs every page he wrote. 'Grete Clerke' as he was, he was never wilfully esoteric: quotations and illusions rose unbidden to the surface of his full and fertile mind, but whether they are to Tristram Shandy or James Thurber they elucidate, not decorate. His works are all of a piece: a book in one genre will correct, illumine or amplify what is latent in another."

Long before Lewis went to Magdalene he had acquired a warm regard for Cambridge. When at 22 he first visited the city he liked the charming little quadrangles "with tiled gables, sun dials, and tall chimneys like Tudor houses. . . . One felt everywhere the touch of Puritanism, of something Whiggish, a little defiant perhaps. . . . Oxford is more magnificent, Cambridge perhaps more intriguing. Our characteristic colour is the pale grey, almost yellow, old stone; theirs the warm brown of old brick." Though he liked the undergraduates he met, he thought the dons inferior to those in Oxford "in charm of manner and geniality."

The greatest glory of Cambridge is King's College Chapel, founded by Henry VI in 1440. Its great fan-vaulted ceiling is unexcelled. On his first visit Lewis, overwhelmed, exclaimed that it was "beautiful beyond hope or belief."

EARLY YEARS. "I was born in the winter of 1898 at Belfast, the son of a solicitor and of a clergyman's daughter," Lewis writes in *Surprised by Joy.* "My father's people were true Welshmen, sentimental, passionate, and rhetorical, easily moved both to anger and to tenderness, men who laughed and cried a great deal and who had not much of the talent for happiness." His mother's people were "a cooler race. Their minds were critical and ironic and they had the talent for happiness in a high degree." He believed himself to have inherited something of both traits.

Some of the warm and meaningful attachments of his life were formed early. Indoors at Little Lea, where the family moved in 1905, he and his older brother Warren were left alone in their chosen attic quarters to write, draw, play games, and make up imaginary worlds to their hearts' content. In a house filled with books the two boys read endlessly. When the weather was good, they would venture long distances from home on their bicycles. During this time Lewis discovered an Irish companion named Arthur Greeves, whose tastes were almost identical to his own. They walked the woodlands, fields, and rocky roads around Belfast together, talking about Scandinavian mythology, and in 1914 began a correspondence that was to last until Lewis's death in 1963.

The elusive joy of Lewis's early life was tempered by sorrow. At ten he saw his mother lie dying of cancer. Later he experienced a growing antipathy to his father, not because he was treated badly by him, but because of his parent's uniquely disjointed manner of thought. Sometimes their attempts to communicate with their father left the two sons hilarious; other times it left them angry.

Sent to boarding school in England at ten years, Lewis did not realize that he would never again live in Ireland except for brief intervals. One such interval was in 1929 when Warren was in China, and Lewis returned to Belfast to be with his father during his last illness. Thereafter he visited Ireland on vacations only.

Little Lea, 1919

Belfast from the Holywood Hills

The northward prospect across Belfast Lough: "One of those great contrasts which have bitten deeply into my mind — Niflheim and Asgard, Britain and Logres, Handramit and Harandra, air and ether, the low world and the high. . . ."

"Already one's mind dwells upon the sights and sounds and smells of home; the distant murmurings of 'the Yards', the broad sweep of the Lough, the noble front of Cave Hill and the fragrant little glens and breezy meadows of our own hills. And the sea! I cannot bear to live too far away from it. At Belfast, whether hidden or in sight, still it dominates the general impression of nature's face lending its own crisp flavour to the winds and its own subtle magic to horizons, even when they conceal it."

Little Lea, 1905

Often confined inside by the Irish weather, Warren Lewis says, "we always had pencils, paper, chalk, and paint-boxes, and this recurring imprisonment gave us occasion and stimulus to develop the habit of creative imagination. We learnt to draw; my brother made his first attempts at writing; together we devised the imaginary country of 'Boxen', which proliferated hugely and became our solace and joy for many years to come."

Little Lea today

Belfast Lough, the Antrim Mountains, and Cave Hill from the attic window of Little Lea

Family picture, about 1900. Front row: Flora Lewis (mother); Warren H. Lewis; grandfather; Cousin Irene; Aunt Agnes; C. S. Lewis. Back row: Albert James Lewis (father); grandmother

Lewis as a baby

*His mother, Flora
Augusta Hamilton Lewis*

*His father,
Albert James Lewis*

In his autobiography, Lewis wrote that in the attic at Little Lea, "my first stories were written and illustrated, with enormous satisfaction. They were an attempt to combine my two chief literary pleasures — 'dressed animals' and 'knights in armor.' As a result, I wrote about chivalrous mice and rabbits who rode out in complete mail to kill not giants but cats." Not only did he enjoy writing stories, but he also liked to compile them into books. The annotations on the excerpts shown in this section were later added by Lewis himself. "Leborough" refers to Little Lea.

Take any suby ...

THE ONE⁻ THIEF.

OILE

MOUSE GOBLET
TIME OF BUNNY I

"The Animal-Land which came into action in the holidays when my brother was at home was a modern Animal-Land; it had to have trains and steamships if it was to be a country shared with him. It followed, of course, that the medieval Animal-Land about which I wrote my stories must be the same country at an earlier period; and of course the two periods must be properly connected. This led me from romancing to historiography; I set about writing a full history of Animal-Land. Though more than one version of this instructive work is extant, I never succeeded in bringing it down to modern times; centuries take a deal of filling when all the events have to come out of the historian's head."

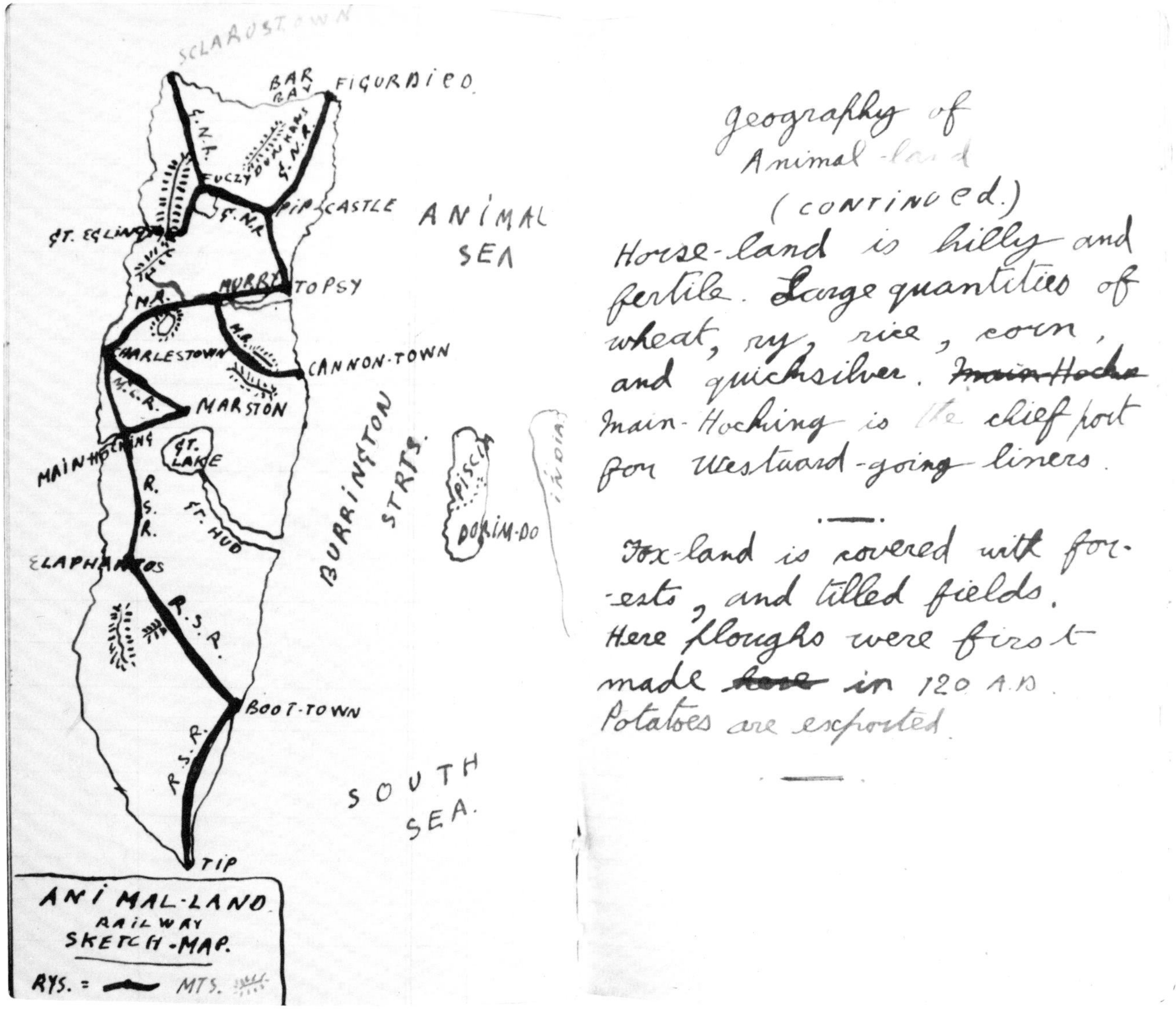

Map labels (handwritten):
SCLARUSTOWN · BAR BAY · FIGURDIEO · ANIMAL SEA · S.Z.T. · S.N.R. · FUCZYDOWNRAL · S.N.R. · PIR-CASTLE · GT. EGLING · S.N.R. · HUBBY · TOPSY · N.R. · N.R. · CHARLESTOWN · CANNON-TOWN · MARSTON · BURRINGTON STRTS. · PISCIA · DORIM-DO · VIOLA · GT. LAKE · MAIN-HOCKING · R.S.R. · ST. HUD · ELAPHANTOS · R.S.R. · R.S.R. · BOOT-TOWN · R.S.R. · SOUTH SEA. · TIP

ANIMAL-LAND
RAILWAY
SKETCH-MAP.
RYS. = ⎯⎯ MTS. ⦀⦀⦀

geography of Animal-land

(continued.)

Horse-land is hilly and fertile. Large quantities of wheat, rye, rice, corn, and quicksilver. ~~Main-Hocke~~ Main-Hocking is the chief port for westward-going liners.

Fox-land is covered with forests, and tilled fields. Here ploughs were first made ~~here~~ in 120 A.D. Potatoes are exported.

"From history it was only a step to geography. There was soon a map of Animal-Land — several maps, all tolerably consistent. Then Animal-Land had to be geographically related to my brother's India, and India consequently lifted out of its place in the real world. We made it an island, with its north coast running along the back of the Himalayas; between it and Animal-Land my brother rapidly invented the principal steamship routes."

Plate VIII

Theodore.   Sir Goose.   General Quickstepppe.
Sir Chas. Arabudda. Mr. Reginald Vant. H.M. The Rajah. Viscount Puddiph
                                                                      I-st

Water-colour drawing of the Jolly of the
                                                    1910
House, by C. S. Lewis.   1904.

Plate XVII

General Quickstepppe.   An hussar.

Colonel Fortescue

Ink drawing of the interior of a Piscian State
Railway Saloon, and a head enlarged
from it; by C. S. Lewis.   1910.

"And those parts of that world which we regarded as our own
— Animal-Land and India — were increasingly peopled with
consistent characters."

Plate XL

Water-colour and ink drawing of ruins of the first united Boxonian Parliament House in Piscia, by C. S. Lewis. Early, but not primitive. Rediscovered 1926 and dated conjecturally 1907 (?)

As their history went on, Animal-Land and India were united into the single state of Boxen. "By a wise provision they retained their separate kings but had a common legislative assembly, the Damerfesk. . . . The electoral system was democratic, but this mattered very much less than in England, for the Damerfesk was never doomed to one fixed meeting place. The joint sovereigns could summon it anywhere, say at the tiny fishing village of Danphabel . . . or on the island of Piscia. . . . The records sometimes call this assembly the Parliament, but that is misleading. It had only a single chamber, and the kings presided."

Plate XXXV

Water colour drawing of the Little Master, by C.S. Lewis, rediscovered 1920, with the preceding.

1907-8 (?)

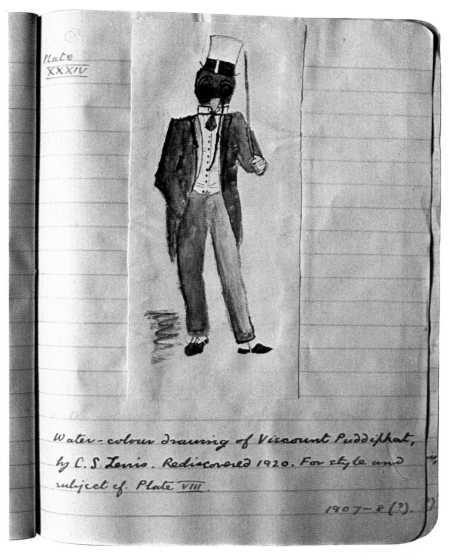

Plate XXXIV

Water-colour drawing of Viscount Puddiphat, by C.S. Lewis. Rediscovered 1920. For style and subject cf. Plate VIII

1907-8 (?)

The kings, however, yielded their effective control to a functionary known as the Littlemaster, "a Prime Minister, a judge, and if not always Commander-in-Chief . . . certainly always a member of the General Staff." One of the Littlemasters was a frog named Lord John Big, who "brought to his task one rather unfair advantage: he had been the tutor of the two young kings and continued to hold over them a quasi-parental authority.

. . . Lord Big, immense in size, resonant of voice, chivalrous (he was the hero of innumerable duels), stormy, eloquent, and impulsive, almost was the state. The two sovereigns who allowed themselves to be dominated by Lord Big were King Benjamin VII of Animal-Land [a rabbit] and Rajah Hawki VI of India." Viscount Puddiphat, an owl, was a music-hall artist of Boxen.

I.   *To Mars and back.* - Lewis

When I first met Brown F.R.A.S., I had no idea that his love for Jules Verne's side of astronomy would lead me into this. I came to know him through his ½-brother Jeames: as I took a mild interest in astronomy, Brown and I were good chums. It was after I had known him for about a month that he suddenly dropped in to see me one night.

"Bensin I'm going to Mars" he said in his short way. I laughed. "How?" said I. "In a vessel" said he "all I want is money." "Don't be a fool Brown" said I "you'll never do it." "Oh yes I will" quoth he "at any rate I'll try."

"It is wrong to commit suicide, especially when one has wife and children" I observed.

"It is, very wrong," said Brown "but I am not going to." However I thought I'd give you the chance of coming with me: — will you?"

Come with him! — I hadn't thought of that. I reflected and then said,

"If you don't mind Brown I'll wait till you have settled your arrangements"

"Sorry Bensin" returned my friend "but I am going to start from central Africa. I sail from Southampton to-morrow night!"

"Well I'll come, and tell you what I'm going to, in the morning. said I

"Right. good by said he
   good by said I
   and he went.

"The idea of other planets exercised . . . a peculiar, heady attraction, which was quite different from any other of my literary interests. Most emphatically it was not the romantic spell of *Das Ferne*. 'Joy' (in my technical sense) never darted from Mars or the Moon. This was something coarser and stronger. The interest, when the fit was upon me, was ravenous, like a lust."

Plate **XX**

Head of Sigdon

A head of Lord Peabody

Sigdon
Efrit3

Peabody
Jordan.

Ink drawings of four characters from the
"Game of War", by C. S. Lewis   1912

Plate **XIX**

Ink drawing of a sunset with dying war-
rior, by C. S. Lewis.
1913.

Other stories written during Lewis's school years in England

105

Lewis's first experience with English schooling was at Wynyard, in Watford, Hertfordshire, northwest of London. He described his two years there as "wasted and miserable." Later he attended Campbell College, about a mile from Little Lea. After less than a term he left, due to illness and his father's dissatisfaction with the school, "which had been founded for the express purpose of giving Ulster boys all the advantages of a public-school education without the trouble of crossing the Irish Sea."

Like these brothers, the two Lewis brothers crossed the Irish Sea by ferry from Belfast to Liverpool to attend school in England. Since it was a trip he took six times a year, Lewis later wrote that his mind was "stored with ship's-side images to a degree unusual for such an untravelled man."

Shortly after his twelfth birthday Lewis returned to England, where he spent two years at Cherbourg House, a preparatory school in Malvern subsequently renamed Ellerslie. "[It] was a smallish school with less than twenty boarders. . . . Here indeed my education really began."

Illustrations by Arthur Rackham in Siegfried and the Twilight of the Gods

A casual reading of a literary periodical in a schoolroom at Cherbourg House set off a renaissance in Lewis's inner life. "What I had read was the words *Siegfried and the Twilight of the Gods*. What I had seen was one of Arthur Rackham's illustrations to that volume. I had never heard of Wagner, nor of Siegfried. I thought the twilight of the gods meant the twilight in which the gods lived. How did I know, at once and beyond question, that this was no Celtic or silvan or terrestrial twilight? But so it was. Pure 'Northernness' engulfed me: a vision of huge, clear spaces hanging above the Atlantic in the endless twilight of Northern summer, remoteness, severity, . . . and almost at the same moment I knew that I had met this before, long, long ago."

Malvern College

While Lewis was attending Cherbourg House, Warren was down the hill at Malvern College. Lewis regarded the prospect of attending the "Coll" with excitement. "The crowd of boys older than oneself, their dazzling air of sophistication, scraps of their esoteric talk overheard, were like Park Lane in the old 'Season' to a girl who is to be a debutante next year. . . . The whole school was a great temple for the worship of these mortal gods; and no boy ever went there more prepared to worship them than I." His actual experience at Malvern was less pleasant than he had anticipated. He particularly hated the athletic side of his education there: "My native clumsiness, combined with the lack of early training . . . had ruled out all possibility of my ever playing well enough to amuse myself, let alone to satisfy other players. I accepted games (quite a number of boys do) as one of the necessary evils of life, comparable to Income Tax or the Dentist."

Harry Wakelyn Smith ("Smewgy"), whose portrait hangs in this Malvern classroom, was described by Lewis as one of his two greatest teachers. "He first taught me the right sensuality of poetry, how it should be savored and mouthed in solitude. . . . Nor had I ever met before perfect courtesy in a teacher. It had nothing to do with softness; Smewgy could be very severe, but it was the severity of a judge, weighty and measured, without taunting."

Carpe Diem

When, in haughty exultation thou durst laugh in Fortune's face

Or when thou hast sunk down weary, trampled in the ceaseless race,

Dellius!, think on this I pray thee; but the twinkling of an eye,

May endure thy pain or pleasure; for, thou knowest, thou shalt die,

Whether on some breeze-kissed upland with a flask of mellow wine

Thou hast all the world forgotten, stretched beneath the friendly pine,

Or, in foolish toil consuming all the springtime of thy life,

Thou hast worked for useless silver and endured the bitter strife:

Still unchanged thy doom remaineth. Thou art set towards thy goal,

Out into the empty breezes soon shall flicker forth thy soul.

Here, then, by the plashing streamlet, fill the tinkling glass, I pray,

Hither bring the short-lived garlands, and be happy — for to-day.

C. S. Lewis.

Lewis's poem "Carpe Diem," written during his days at Malvern, differs from his later efforts by its classical style and pessimistic tone. Along with other distinguished student writing efforts, it was recorded in the headmaster's book.

C. S. Lewis.
English Poem "Carpe Diem".
Oct. 13. 1913.

V. C. Hemsley.
L. J. Part I. $\frac{152}{156}$.

C. Mattox
L.T. Part I. $\frac{149}{156}$. 1st Term

Lewis's dormitory at Malvern

After a distinguished career as teacher of English at Malvern, George Sayer is now Librarian and Director of the Resources Area. He was once a favorite pupil of Lewis at Oxford

Hallway at Malvern

In spite of his academic success here, Lewis wrote home in March 1914, imploring his father to take him away. His brother Warren commented: "Much to my surprise, my father reacted to this letter by making an immediate and sensible decision: Jack was to leave Malvern at the end of the school year. . . . The fact is that he should never have been sent to a public school at all. Already, at fourteen, his intelligence was such that he would have fitted in better among undergraduates than among schoolboys; and by his temperament he was bound to be a misfit, a heretic, an object of suspicion within the collective-minded and standardising Public School system."

Relieved at having left Malvern, Lewis spent two exciting years in Bookham under the rigid tutoring of W. T. Kirkpatrick, the "Great Knock." Their first conversation as Kirkpatrick met him at the railway station set the tone for the months ahead: "I began to 'make conversation' in the deplorable manner which I had acquired at those evening parties [in Belfast]. . . . I said I was surprised at the 'scenery' of Surrey; it was 'wilder' than I had expected. 'Stop!' shouted Kirk. 'What do you mean by wildness and what grounds had you for not expecting it?' A few passes sufficed to show that I had no clear and distinct idea corresponding to the word 'wildness,' and that, in so far as I had any idea at all, 'wildness' was a singularly inept word."

"It is however no sentiment but plainest fact to say that I owe him in the intellectual sphere as much as one human being can owe another. That he enabled me to win a Scholarship is the least that he did for me. It was an atmosphere of unrelenting clearness and rigid honesty of thought that one breathed from living with him — and this I shall be the better for as long as I live. And if this is the greatest thing, there are others which none of us will forget: his dry humour, his imperturbable good temper, and his amazing energy — these it is good to have seen. . . . The more one sees of weakness, affectation, and general vagueness in the majority of men, the more one admires that rigid, lonely old figure — more like some ancient Stoic standing fast in the Roman decadence than a modern scholar living in the home counties. Indeed we may almost call him a great man."

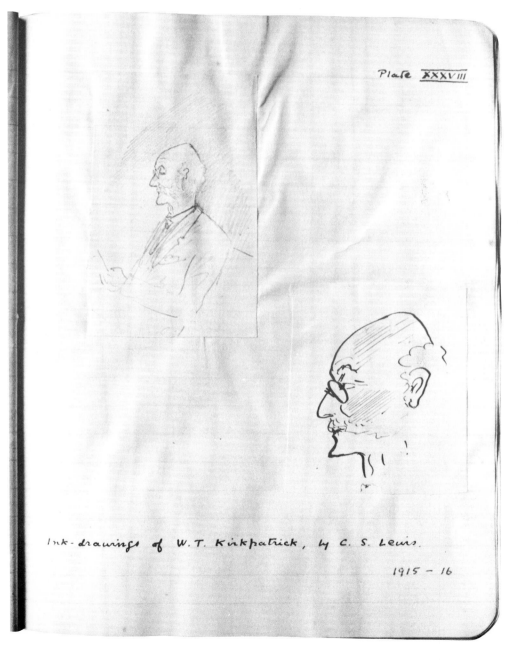

Plate XXXVIII

Ink-drawings of W. T. Kirkpatrick, by C. S. Lewis.

1915 – 16

THE LAND. The raw material on which Lewis's imagination often worked was the land, mostly the British Isles, where he spent his entire life except for a tour of duty in France during World War I and a visit to Greece with Joy late in his life. The way to acquaint oneself with the land is on foot: "I number it among my blessings," he said, "that my father had no car. . . . The deadly power of rushing about wherever I pleased had not been given me. . . . I had not been allowed to deflower the very idea of distance."

Walking through hills and valleys provided the right balance between appreciation and anticipation. "No one can describe the delight of coming to a sudden drop and looking down into a rich wooded valley where you see the roofs of the place where you're going to have supper and bed; especially if the sunset lies on the ridge beyond the valley. There is so much mixed in it; the mere physical anticipation, as of a horse nearing his stable, the sense of accomplishment and the feeling of 'one more

town', one further away into the country you don't know, and the old, never hackneyed romance of travelling."

From the 1920s until 1939, Lewis made an annual walking tour in addition to his daily walks. With mouth closed, not smoking his pipe, and eyes and ears open, he would "take in what is there and give no thought to what might have been there or what is somewhere else."

ONE SUCH WALK made in 1930 took Lewis and three friends — Owen Barfield, Alfred C. Harwood, and Walter O. Field — from Dunster to Challacombe, in Exmoor, southwest England. In a letter to Arthur Greeves he later described this fifty-mile walk.

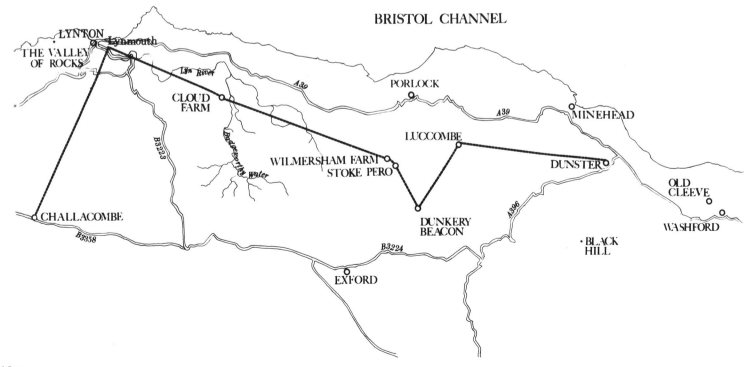

"We motored from Oxford to Dunster, three of us leaving the car about five miles beforehand and the fourth driving on. It was about six when we did so and we therefore had a delightful evening 'prologue' to the whole walk over moors with a ragged sunset ahead of us lighting up the pools — very much like an illustration to Scott. Then down into a steep valley, over a swift stream as broad as Connswater but only an inch or so deep above its rattling pebbles, and so into the broad, empty, practically dark street of Dunster, which stretches up to the castle."

"Next morning there was a thick fog. Some of the others were inclined to swear at it, but I (and I soon converted Barfield) rejoiced to meet the moor at its grimmest. Imagine a wonderful morning following a narrow path alongside of a steep hill with gaunt fir trees looming up suddenly out of the greyness, and sometimes a thinning of the mist that revealed perhaps a corner of a field with drystone wall unexpectedly far beneath us, or a rushing brook, or a horse grazing."

"Then down into greener country and hedges for lunch at the village of Luccombe."

Luccombe

"In the afternoon the fog thickened, but we continued in spite of it to ascend Dunkery Beacon as we had originally intended. There was of course not a particle of view to be seen, and we knew when we had reached the top only by the fact that we could find nothing higher and by the cairn of stones over which the wind was hurrying the fog like smoke from a chimney on a stormy day."

"The descent, largely guided by compass, was even more exciting: especially the suddenness with which a valley broke upon us — one moment nothing but moor and fog: then ghosts of trees all around us: then a roaring of invisible water beneath, and next moment the sight of the stream itself, the blackness of its pools and the whiteness of its rapids seeming to tear holes (as it were) in the neutral grey of the mist."

"We drank tea at the tiny hamlet of Stoke Pero, where there is a little grey church without a tower that holds only about twenty people. Here, according to an excellent custom of our walks, one of the party read us a chapter of Scripture from the lectern while the rest of us sat heavily in the pews and spread out our mackintoshes to let the linings steam off."

"Then after a leisurely walk through woods we reached Wilmersham Farm where we found our car parked in the farmyard, and Field looking out of a window to assure us that there were beds and supper for all. We had a little parlour with a wood stove to ourselves and excellent hot meals and the bedrooms — two in a room — were beautifully clean. We had only made about sixteen miles but were tired enough as it had been very rough country."

127

"Next morning when I woke I was delighted to find the sun streaming through the window. Looking out I found a blue sky: the farmyard, with hens scratching and a cat padding stealthily among them, was bright with sunlight; beyond the long blue grey horizons of the moor rolled up to the sky in every direction."

"This day we made about ten miles by paths across the open moor to a place where we met a road, and there Field met us in the car with lunch. A cold wind was blowing by that time, so we had our meal (as you and I have often done) in the closed car with all windows up and had the sensation of snugness. About 2½ hours after lunch, having done a very tricky walk across heather by pure map reading (no paths) we were relieved to strike the valley of a river called Badgeworthy Water (pronounced Badgerry)."

"A glorious climb, deepening of course as it proceeds, steep-sided, with many rocks in it, and soon with dotted trees that thicken later into woods: not of fir, but of stunted oaks, so gnarled that they give the impression of being in a subterranean forest of sea weed, and the branches often coated with moss to the top. We had to ford the Badgeworthy — not very easy as (like all mountain streams) it will be six inches deep in one place and five feet the next: ice cold and the bottom slippery. Barfield created great amusement by putting his socks in his boots and trying to throw them across a narrow place so that he should not have that encumbrance while wading. Instead they lit in the middle and, after sailing a few yards like high-roofed galleons, lit on the top of a fall where they stuck, rocking with the current and threatening every second to go swirling down to a whirlpool beneath. I, who was already safe on the farther shore, ran down in my bare feet and hooked them to land with a stick. We sat down for about half an hour with our backs against a little cliff of rock, in the sun and out of the wind, to eat chocolate and dry and warm our numbed legs. The first bumble bee buzzed by us. The colours of the stream, broken up by a series of falls above us and floored with green, brown, golden, and red stones, were indescribable."

"When we were dry, we worked our way down valley to Cloud Farm where billets had been secured by Field. Minto, Maureen and I had stayed here about five years before, so I had a great welcome from the farm people. This evening all four of us had a kind of formal philosophical discussion on the good. I shared a room with Barfield and lay awake for a little while, listening to the noise of the stream, which is only about twenty feet from the farm house: and under that noise a profound silence. These Exmoor farms are one of the loveliest habitations you can imagine."

"Next day we walked down the valley of the Lynn and lunched at Lynmouth. The valley is very deep — about 800 feet — and the woods on the sides almost deserve to be called forest. The river — which again we had to wade — is much bigger than the Badgeworthy and so agonisingly cold that at the first shock it's almost the same feeling as stepping into a bath much too hot for you."

"After lunch our route lay along the cliffs and through the Valley of Rocks, which I did not greatly admire: a place of enormous crags *without water* is a little bit horrible. One needs a stream to give these huge carcasses a soul, don't you think?"

"Best of all was after tea, when we struck inland again over the moor in one of those golden evening lights that pours a dreamlike *mildness* over the world. Light seemed to be a liquid that you could drink, and the surrounding peace was, if anything, deepened by the noise and bustle of a fussy little narrow gauge railway, which had a train puffing slowly along it. All its windows turned to gold in the light of the sunset. That night we slept at Challacombe and composed *ex tempore* poetry telling the story of the Fall between us in the metre of *Hiawatha*. We had done well over twenty miles and felt immortal."

"The next day was grey with occasional rain. We got badly lost in some rather forbidding hills and failed to meet Field for lunch, got a lift along a dull stretch of road in a lorry, had tea at South Moulton and motored to Exeter. . . . It was horrid to be in a city again. As Field said, 'After training ourselves for the last few days to notice *everything,* we have now to train ourselves to notice nothing.' Next morning the party broke up, Barfield and Harwood motoring back north, while Field and I trained to Bournemouth."

"NO MAN would find an abiding strangeness in the moon unless he were the sort of man who could find it in his own back garden," Lewis wrote. He was among those who could find it both places. An early longing for what he called Joy had led him to wide reading, had stimulated imaginative boyhood efforts at poetry and adventure, and had developed in him a constant alert receptiveness to the natural world.

As he walked the land throughout his life he was both enjoying nature and storing up future pleasure as images and ideas deposited in his mind. These pictures and thoughts would later appear, ripened, in his writing, whether expository or fictional.

The photographs in this section are of places that Lewis visited, and most of the text is Lewis's own. But the relationship between the two is one of suggestion and interpretation, not of correlation or representation. It is scarcely possible that *this* tree was in Lewis's mind as he wrote *The Magician's Nephew,* but perhaps the photograph captures something of what Lewis once saw, retained in his mind, and later fashioned into a word-picture of the Wood Between the Worlds: "He was standing by the edge of a small pool — not more than ten feet from side to side — in a wood. The trees grew close together and were so leafy that he could get no glimpse of the sky. All the light was green light that came through the leaves: but there must have been a very strong sun overhead, for this green daylight was bright and warm. It was the quietest wood you could possibly imagine. There were no birds, no insects, no animals, and no wind. . . . You could almost feel the trees drinking the water up with their roots."

A walk with Owen Barfield once took Lewis to Derbyshire. "It is appreciably more like my ideal country than any I have yet seen. It is limestone mountains: which means, from the practical point of view, that it has the jagged sky lines and deep valleys of ordinary mountainous country, but with this important difference, that owing to the paleness of the rock and the extreme clarity of the rivers, it is *light* instead of sombre — sublime yet smiling — like the delectable mountains. It gives you something of the same sensation as Blake's songs."

"I gazed down into a little ditch beneath a grey hedge, where there was a pleasant mixture of ivies and low plants and mosses and thought of herbalists and their art, and what a private retired wisdom it would be to go on probing along such hedges and the eaves of woods for some herb of virtuous powers . . . and having at the same time a stronger sense of the mysteries at our feet where homeliness and magic embrace one another."

"Lucy looked very hard at the trees of that glade. 'Why, I do believe they're moving,' she said to herself. 'They're walking about. . . .' And now there was no doubt that the trees were really moving — moving in and out through one another as if in a complicated country dance. . . . The first tree she looked at seemed at first glance to be not a tree at all but a huge man with a shaggy beard and great bushes of hair. She was not frightened: she had seen such things before. But when she looked again he was only a tree though he was still moving. You couldn't see whether he had feet or roots, of course, because when trees move they don't walk on the surface of the earth; they wade in it as we do in water."

Dovedale

Northeast coast, northern Ireland

Without question there is immediate pleasure in experiencing the prodigal glories of nature around us. Lewis suggests there is a further value that comes later, "in the images and ideas which we have put down to mature in the cellarage of our brains, thence to come up with a continually improving bouquet. Already the hills are getting higher, the grass greener, and the sea bluer than they really were; and thanks to the deceptive working of happy memory our poorest stopping places will become haunts of impossible pleasure and Epicurean repast."

141

Northern Ireland

Writing about Lewis's Narnia tales, his biographer Roger Lancelyn Green suggests, "The sense of wonder and discovery, the feeling of awakened memory rather than of cunningly drawn word-pictures, is helped greatly by the description of scenery and of even the smallest facet of nature — always growing naturally out of the narrative and never superimposed. Lewis's long, solitary walks in Ulster and Surrey and in the country round Oxford have borne good fruit in these vivid composite scenes: the love of all the beauties of scenery and nature, flora and fauna, go to their creation — from the mountains of Donegal — 'as near heaven as you can get in Thulcandra' — to the apparently instinctive sympathy with mice or badgers or bears."

On the basis of his acquaintance with Lewis, Father Walter Hooper believes that "if you want to plunge into . . . the very quiddity of some Narnian countryside, you must go to what Lewis considered the loveliest spot he had ever seen. It is in the Carlingford Mountains of southern Ireland."

"And beyond all this . . . so remote that they seem fantastically abrupt, at the very limit of your vision, imagine the mountains. They are no stragglers. They are steep and compact and pointed and toothed and jagged. They seem to have nothing to do with the little hills and cottages that divide you from them. And sometimes they are blue, sometimes violet; but quite often they look transparent — as if huge sheets of gauze had been cut out into mountainous shapes and hung up there, so that you could see through them the light of the invisible sea at their backs."

Looking at the Mourne Mountains, from Carlingford

144

St. John's Point, County Donegal

"You know that none loves the hills of Down (or of Donegal) better than I: and indeed, partly from interest in Yeats and Celtic mythology, partly from a natural repulsion to noisy drum-beating bullying orangemen and partly from association with Butler, I begin to have a very warm feeling for Ireland in general."

Lewis preferred to vacation in out-of-the-way places not likely to appear in travel folders. He became known as the famous summer visitor in this richly Neolithic and wild area in the vicinity of Inver, County Donegal on the Atlantic coast. "It continues cold (you would think it Arctic) here and wet, but with lovely gleams at times in which far-off mountains show three times their real height and with a radiance that suggests Bunyan's 'delectable mountains.' . . . P.S. I doubt if you'll find any Leprechauns in Eire now. The Radio has driven them away."

Inver area, County Donegal

"All the mountains look like mountains in a story, and there are wooded valleys, and golden sands, and the smell of peat from every cottage."

County Donegal

"I have seen landscapes . . . which, under a particular light, made me feel that at any moment a giant might raise his head over the next ridge. Nature has that in her which compels us to invent giants: and only giants will do."

Northwest County Donegal

Muckish Gap, County Donegal

150

Claghaneely, County Donegal

North shore, County Donegal

"I have been in really quiet and unearthly spots in my native Ireland. I stayed for a fortnight in a bungalow which none of the peasants will approach at night because the desolate coast on which it stands is haunted by 'the good people'. There is also a ghost but (and this is interesting) they don't seem to mind *him;* the faeries are a more serious danger."

County Donegal, the Bloody Foreland area

Ancient monuments, such as this plundered Megalithic tomb at Malin More, County Donegal, and standing stones dot the landscape of both Ireland and England. Their opaque mysteries of druids and ancient religious rites greatly fascinated Lewis.

Stone fences often surround the fields and form the hiking paths in northwest Ireland.

Muckish Gap, County Donegal

"Of landscapes, as of people, one becomes more tolerant after one's twentieth year. . . . We learn to look at them, not *in the flat* but *in depth,* as things to be burrowed into. It is not merely a question of lines and colours but of smells, sounds and tastes as well; I often wonder if professional artists don't lose something of the real love of earth by seeing it in eye-sensations only?"

The Thames River

Along the Ridge Way, Berkshire

"Around us and to our left the country had all the same character; close, smooth grass, deliciously springy to the foot; chalk showing through here and there and making the few ploughed places almost cream colour; and, about three to the mile, clumps of fir whose darkness made them stand out very strikingly from the low tones of the ground."

you sympathise with me? Pray for me to all your gods and goddesses 'like a good man! No the Meagre One was not born with a squint: but long, long, long, ago, so *long ago that Stonehenge had a roof and walls & was a new built temple, he killed a spider. The good people of his day, outraged at this barbarity, stuck a dagger thro' his nerve centre which paralyzed him without making him unconscious, seated him on the altar at St. Henge's temple & locked him up with the spiders son. The latter began to spin

PROBLEM A
To raise the Meagre
One.
A = the student
B. = the M.O.

a solid mass of cobweb from the opposite corner. Very very slowly through countless years the web grew while the poor meagre One—who couldn't die—developped a squint from watching it getting nearer. At last after countless ages stonehenge disappeared under an enormous mass of web & remained thus till one day Merlin happenned to set a match to it and so discover what was inside: hence the myth of Merlin's having "built" St. Henge's To this day if you go there at sunrise & run round it 7 times, looking over your shoulder you can see again the wretched prisoner trying to "struggle" as the horrid sticky stands close round him. Cheap excursion trains are run for those who wish to try it [SEE FIGURE] The Tales of a Grandfather

Lewis was fascinated by the ancient monument of Stonehenge, near Amesbury, Wiltshire. He shared with Greeves some antic speculation about its early days in this 1916 letter.

"I was always involuntarily looking for scenes that might belong to the Wagnerian world, here a steep hillside covered with firs where Mime might meet Sieglinde, there a sunny glade where Siegfried might listen to the bird, or presently a dry valley of rocks where the lithe scaly body of Fafner might emerge from its cave. But soon . . . nature ceased to be a mere reminder of the books, became herself the medium of the real joy. . . . It was the mood of a scene that mattered to me; and in tasting that mood my skin and nose were as busy as my eyes."

Savernake Forest, Wiltshire

160

Stone circle at Avebury, Wiltshire

In *The Horse and His Boy,* Shasta came to the tombs of the ancient kings, which were on the edge of the desert just outside the gates of Tashbaan: "great masses of mouldering stone shaped like gigantic bee-hives, but a little narrower. They looked very black and grim, for the sun was now setting right behind them. . . . Now that Shasta knew he would have to spend the night alone he began to like the look of the place less and less. There was something very uncomfortable about those great, silent shapes of stone. He had been trying his hardest for a long time not to think of ghouls: but he couldn't keep it up any longer."

161

"I . . . notice smaller things much more than I did, which is a great advantage in what we ordinarily call dull country. A flower or the turning of a stream can now make up for the lack of mountains and woods."

"Say your prayers in a garden early, ignoring steadfastly the dew, the birds and the flowers, and you will come away overwhelmed by its freshness and joy; go there in order to be overwhelmed and, after a certain age, nine times out of ten nothing will happen to you."

In *The Horse and His Boy* Lewis describes a setting in which Shasta and Bree find themselves. "Behind them lay a little copse. Before them the turf, dotted with white flowers, sloped down to the brow of a cliff. Far below them, so that the sound of the breaking waves was very faint, lay the sea. Shasta had never seen it from such a height and never seen so much of it before, nor dreamed how many colours it had."

Zennor Head, Cornwall

Tintagel

"The show parts of Cornwall — the parts one has read about — are all on the coast. We lay this night at Tintagel, storied name. There is a generally diffused belief that this place is connected with King Arthur; so far as I know from Malory, Layamon, and Geoffrey of Monmouth, it is not; it is really the seat of King Mark and the Tristam story."

Cornwall coast, near St. Ives

"A true philosophy may sometimes validate an experience of nature; an experience of nature cannot validate a philosophy. . . . Nature never taught me that there exists a God of glory and of infinite majesty. I had to learn that in other ways. But nature gave the word *glory* a meaning for me. I still do not know where else I could have found one. I do not see how the 'fear' of God could have ever meant to me anything but the lowest prudential efforts to be safe, if I had never seen certain ominous ravines and unapproachable crags."

Perranporth Beach, Cornwall

"I remember, in particular, glorious hours of bathing.... It was surf bathing: not the formal affair with boards that you have now, but mere rough and tumble, in which the waves, the monstrous, emerald, deafening waves, are always the winner, and it is at once a joke, a terror, and a joy to look over your shoulder and see (too late) one breaker of such sublime proportions that you would have avoided him had you known he was coming. But they gather themselves up, pre-eminent above their fellows, as suddenly and unpredictably as a revolution."

In 1933 Lewis with his brother made a trip to southwestern Scotland, a part of the British Isles that he did not often visit. They had "one day's glorious walk on the shores of Loch Long and Lomond and across the mountains between."

Loch Long

"The actual beach of Loch Lomond pleased me very much —
an ordinary pebbly beach such as you might find at the sea with
the unusual addition that it had trees on it and that you could
drink the water."

The mountains between Loch Long and Loch Lomond "seemed to me to excel all other mountains in one respect — the curiously fantastic, yet heavy, shapes of rock into which the summits are formed. They realise one's ideas of mountains as the fastnesses of the giants."

"Up in the mountains we had a glorious hour at a stream — a golden brown stream, with cataracts and deep pools. We spread out all our clothes (sweat-sodden) to dry on the flat stones, and lay down in a pool just under a little waterfall, and let the foam come down the back of our heads and round our necks. Then when we were really cool, we came out and sat naked to eat our sandwiches, with our feet still in the rushing water."

In *Reflections on the Psalms* Lewis quotes with obvious delight from Psalm 65: "Thou art good to the earth. . . thou waterest her furrows . . . thou makest it soft with the drops of rain . . . the little hills shall rejoice on every side . . . the valleys shall stand so thick with corn that they shall laugh and sing."

Glen Douglas, Scotland

"Lincoln itself is quite the best cathedral city I have ever seen. The centre of the town, where the cathedral stands, is on the only hill for miles and the cathedral consequently dominates the whole countryside. The surroundings of the cathedral are magnificent — a beautiful close, a castle and a Roman wall."

The Thames near Radcot, Oxfordshire

Wye River Valley, south Wales

"But for our body one whole realm of God's glory — all that we receive through the senses — would go unpraised. For the beasts can't appreciate it and the angels are, I suppose, pure intelligences. They *understand* colours and tastes better than our greatest scientists; but have they retinas or palates? I fancy the 'beauties of nature' are a secret God has shared with us alone. That may be one of the reasons why we were made — and why the resurrection of the body is an important doctrine."

Lewis's personal physician Dr. Robert Havard recalls an excursion to explore the mountains in the Cader Idris area of western Wales with Lewis. "[His] dislike of heights prevented him tackling a steepish slope to the summit. So we separated and he explored a narrow track round a mountain tarn. Apart from this phobia he enjoyed mountains and was a tireless walker."

Western Wales

"All you have heard about Old Narnia is true. It is not the land of Men. It is the country of Aslan, the country of the Walking Trees and Visible Naiads, of Fauns and Satyrs, of Dwarfs and Giants, of the gods and the Centaurs, of Talking Beasts."

Tintern Abbey, southeast Wales

"It is an abbey practically intact except that the roof is gone, and the glass out of the windows, and the floor, instead of a pavement, is a trim green lawn. Anything like the *sweetness* and peace of the long shafts of sunlight falling through the windows on the grass cannot be imagined. All churches should be roofless. A holier place I never saw."

Conway Castle, northwest Wales

The Narnia castles draw from features of many of the castles in the British Isles, such as this fourteenth-century one visited by Lewis with Roger Lancelyn Green. "The castle of Cair Paravel on its little hill towered up above them; before them were the sands, with rocks and little pools of salt water, and sea weed, and the smell of the sea, and long miles of bluish-green waves breaking forever and ever on the beach."

179

"But just where the land of Narnia met the sea . . . there was something on a little hill, shining. It was shining because it was a castle and of course the sunlight was reflected from all the windows which looked towards Peter and the sunset; but to Peter it looked like a great star resting on the seashore."

Dolwyddelan, Wales

"Think of yourself just as a seed patiently waiting in the earth; waiting to come up a flower in the Gardener's good time, up into the real world, the real waking. I suppose that our whole present life, looked back on from there, will seem only a drowsy half-waking. We are here in the land of dreams. But cockcrow is coming. It is nearer now than when I began this letter."

AFTERWORD. C. S. Lewis died on November 22, 1963, one week before his sixty-fifth birthday. The funeral was quiet, only a few persons present in his parish church. Warren Lewis chose the inscription for his brother's gravestone to express his own grief. He identifies its source and special family meaning: "When our mother died on August 23, 1908, there was a Shakespearean calendar hanging on the wall of the room where she died, and my father preserved for the rest of his life the leaf for that day, with its quotation: 'Men must endure their going hence.' "

Headington Quarry Parish Church, Oxfordshire

Father R. E. Head, Vicar, Headington Quarry Parish Church

Roger Lancelyn Green, a student of Lewis at Oxford and later a walking-companion of his, pursued interests in imaginative and romantic literature and myth to become one of the leading advocates of quality in children's literature in the English-speaking world. He is Lewis's biographer, and has written about Lewis's teaching that he "proved to be one of the most successful and stimulating tutors of his time, and his lectures were for some years the most popular in Oxford, certainly in the English School. . . . Lewis surpassed [his closest rivals] both as a sheer transmitter of knowledge in a form so interesting that many students attended the same course of lectures more than once for the fascination of what he told, and the admirable and amusing way in which it was 'put across.'"

A trustee of the Lewis literary estate and the editor of several volumes of essays, poems, and short stories by Lewis, Father Walter Hooper has written: "Lewis tossed almost every copy of his own books, and all his contributions to periodicals, in the 'W.P.B.', as he called it. And just as promptly forgot what he had written. When I became his secretary, I had already compiled an enormous collection of his writings. I showed Lewis my bibliography, which surprised him. 'Did *I* write all these?' he asked, and thereafter named me his Pseudo-Dionysius on the grounds that I had invented most of them. . . . And yet Lewis had a marvellous memory. Following his retirement from Cambridge, he sent me to Magdalene College with seven pages of instructions about the care and disposal of every book in his library. The only order respecting his own works was 'All my own books W.P.B. or apply to your own use.' Needless to say, the W.P.B. went empty."

The Silver Chair: The giant king and queen of Harfang with their court looking at Puddleglum, Scrubb, and Jill.

Having seen a few of Pauline Baynes's illustrations, Lewis asked her to become the illustrator of the Narnia books. When he had looked at her drawings for *The Horse and His Boy,* he wrote her, "It is delightful to find (and not only for selfish reasons) that you do each book a little bit better than the last — it is nice to see an artist growing. . . . Thanks enormously for all the intense work you have put into them all. And more power to your elbow."

The Horse and His Boy: Shasta among the tombs.

186

After Lewis's death, his brother and several close friends select-
ed from his library the books they wanted. The remainder was
purchased by Wroxton College in Oxfordshire, a branch of
Fairleigh Dickinson University in New Jersey, for use in their
special study program in English Literature.

1530 [Henry VIII]

Anon.: Everyman: a moral play [n.d.; between 1510–30].
Colet (d. 1519): Sermon made to the Convocation at Paulis [n.d.].
Poyntz, Sir Francis (d. 1528): Trs. Tables of Cebes the Philosopher. P
Tyndale, William: Trs. Pentateuch [pub. abroad; n.d.: see 1525, 1531].
  Practice of Prelates [pub. abroad]. P

Cardinal Wolsey d.

1531

Golden Litany in English.
Elyot (1490?): The Boke named the Governour. P
Tyndale, William: Trs. Book of Jonah [pub. abroad: see 1525, 1530].
  Answer to Sir Thomas More's Dialogue [pub. abroad; n.d.: see More 1529].

Ulrich Zwingli d.

1532

Chaucer (d. 1400): Works ed. William Thynne [all genuine works hitherto pub. or unpub., and the following that are spurious: Testament of Cresseid (by Henryson); Flower of Courtesie and Complaint of the Black Knight (Lydgate); Testament of Love (Thomas Usk); Letter of Cupid (Occleve); Cuckoo and Nightingale (Sir Thomas Clanvowe?); La Belle Dame sans Mercie (Sir Richard Ross); Assembly of Ladies (unknown); Lamentation of Mary Magdalen (unknown), and others.
  Later edd. of Works with spurious poems added: ed. Thynne (Plowman's Tale) 1542, 1545 (?); ed. Stow (Court of Love and some short poems) 1561; ed. Speght (Flower and the Leaf, Jack Upland, Chaucer's A.B.C., and a new Chaucer's Dream) 1598, 1602, 1687; ed. Urry (Tale of Gamelyn, Pardoner and the Tapster, and Second Merchants Tale) 1721.
  Modern edd. of Works: ed. Singer 1822, Morris 1866, Skeat 1894–7, Pollard 1897].
Elyot (1490?): Pasquil the Plaine. P
Henryson (d. 1500): Testament of Cresseid [in Works of Chaucer above]. V
Hervet, Gentian: Trs. Xenophon's Treatise of Household. P
Lydgate (d. 1450): Flower of Courtesie, Complaint of the Black Knight [in Works of Chaucer above]. V
More (1478): Confutation of Tyndale's Answer [Second Part of Confutation 1533]. P

Henry VIII divorces Katherine of Aragon.
'Natura Brevium' in English.
Rabelais, 'Pantagruel', bk. i (bk. ii called Gargantua 1534, bk. iii 1545, bk. iv 1548–52, bk. v (of doubtful authenticity) 1562–4).
Ariosto, 'Orlando Furioso' (in final form: see 1516).
Machiavelli, 'Il Principe'.
Erasmus, 'Apophthegmata'.

4035   9   C

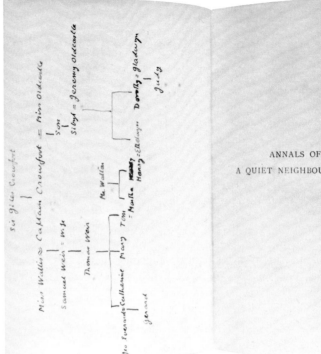

Lewis annotated the books he owned, particularly when he regarded them of special significance to his Christian life or scholarly interests. He inscribed a copy of his first book, *Spirits in Bondage*, to his father. "Built the Promenade" refers, according to Major W. H. Lewis, to a time before his brother knew how to write, and dictated stories to his father on Saturday evenings. "For some reason or other Jack's sentence 'They got an iron pad, they built a promenade' lingered on in the family memory long after this phase of Jack's was forgotten."

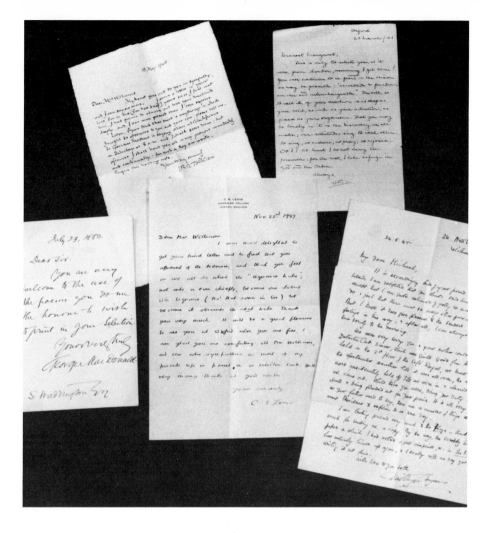

At Wheaton College in Illinois a Lewis Collection was established in 1965, honoring C. S. Lewis and six other writers — J. R. R. Tolkien, Charles Williams, Dorothy Sayers, Owen Barfield, G. K. Chesterton, and George MacDonald. The collection now holds numerous manuscripts, letters, and first editions by these writers as well as published and unpublished studies about them. Dr. Clyde S. Kilby, Curator of the Lewis Collection, is shown here with two students in the room that houses these documents. A sampling of the original letters in the collection is also pictured.

Since 1964 an annual summer gathering at Oxford University has brought together former colleagues of Lewis in Oxford and Cambridge, and friends and admirers. The 1972 gathering was held at Magdalen College.

The toastmaster is Lewis's colleague Colin Hardie, and Father Walter Hooper stands with him.

Sources

9 *Surprised by Joy*, Harcourt Brace Jovanovich, p. 115
10 *Letters of C. S. Lewis*, Harcourt Brace Jovanovich, p. 42
11 *Ibid.*, p. 92
12 *Pilgrim's Regress* (3rd edition), Wm. B. Eerdmans Publishing Company, p. 10
16 *The Silver Chair*, The Macmillan Company, p. 153
17 Unpublished letters to Arthur Greeves, 1916
17 *Surprised by Joy*, Harcourt Brace and Jovanovich, p. 69
18 Unpublished letter to Arthur Greeves, June 1918
18 *Surprised by Joy*, Harcourt Brace and Jovanovich, p. 214
19 *Ibid.*, p. 215
20 *Ibid.*, p. 224
20-21 Unpublished letter to Arthur Greeves, January 10, 1932
24 Unpublished letter to Arthur Greeves, May 9, 1917
28 *Letters of C. S. Lewis*, Harcourt Brace and Jovanovich, p. 104
30 *Ibid.*
32 *Light on C. S. Lewis*, Harcourt Brace and Jovanovich, pp. 60ff.
34 Unpublished letter to Arthur Greeves, undated
37 *Ibid.*, February, 1919
40 *Letters of C. S. Lewis*, Harcourt Brace and Jovanovich, p. 16
42 *Ibid.*, p. 125
44 *Surprised by Joy*, Harcourt Brace and Jovanovich, pp. 199-200
45 *Ibid.*, p. 207
46 *Ibid.*, p. 212
46 *Light on C. S. Lewis*, Harcourt Brace and Jovanovich, p. 54
48 *Letters of C. S. Lewis*, Harcourt Brace and Jovanovich, p. 206
49 *Ibid.*, p. 197
49 *Ibid*, pp. 13ff.
51 *Ibid.*, p. 145
52 *Time and Tide*, August 14, 1954, pp. 1082-1083
53 *Surprised by Joy*, Harcourt Brace and Jovanovich, p. 216
54 *Letters of C. S. Lewis*, p. 111
56 *In Fifty-Two: A Journal of Books and Authors*, Spring, 1964
58 Unpublished letter to Arthur Greeves, undated
62 *Ibid.*
63 *Surprised by Joy*, Harcourt Brace and Jovanovich, p. 13
65 *Light on C. S. Lewis*, Harcourt Brace and Jovanovich, p. 63
67 *Imagination and the Spirit*, Wm. B. Eerdmans Publishing Company, p. 315
70 Unpublished letter to Arthur Greeves, June 26, 1931
71 *Letters to Malcolm*, Harcourt Brace and Jovanovich, p. 91

72 *Letters of C. S. Lewis*, Harcourt Brace and Jovanovich, p. 262
73 *Out of the Silent Planet*, The Macmillan Company, p. 164
74 Unpublished letter to Arthur Greeves, undated
75 *Ibid.*, June, 1930
76 *Ibid.*, undated
77 *Surprised by Joy*, Harcourt Brace and Jovanovich, p. 199
78 *Letters to an American Lady*, Wm. B. Eerdmans Publishing Company, p. 34
78 *Letters of C. S. Lewis*, Harcourt Brace and Jovanovich, p. 265
84 Telecast by Dr. R. W. Ladborough on Anglia Television, Norwich
85 J. A. W. Bennett, *The Humane Medievalist: An Inaugural Address*, pp. 26-27
87 *Letters of C. S. Lewis*, Harcourt Brace and Jovanovich, p. 52
90 *Surprised by Joy*, Harcourt Brace and Jovanovich, p. 11
92 *Ibid.*, p. 154
93 Letter to Arthur Greeves, 1915
94 *Letters of C. S. Lewis*, Harcourt Brace and Jovanovich, p. 1
98 *Surprised by Joy*, Harcourt Brace and Jovanovich, p. 13
99 *Ibid.*
100 *Ibid.*
101 *Ibid.*, p. 14
102 *Ibid.*, p. 79
103 *Ibid.*, pp. 80-81
104 *Ibid.*, p. 35
106 *Ibid.*, pp. 49-50
107 *Ibid.*, p. 143
108 *Ibid.*, p. 58
109 *Ibid.*, pp. 72-73
111 *Ibid.*, pp. 83, 90
112 *Ibid.*, p. 111
115 *Letters of C. S. Lewis*, Harcourt Brace and Jovanovich, pp. 4-5
116 *Surprised by Joy*, Harcourt Brace and Jovanovich, pp. 133ff.
117 *Letters of C. S. Lewis*, Harcourt Brace and Jovanovich, p. 54
118 *Surprised by Joy*, Harcourt Brace and Jovanovich, pp. 149-150
118 *Ibid.*
118 *Ibid.*, p. 146
119-135 Unpublished letter to Arthur Greeves, May, 1930
136 *Ibid.*
137 *Of Other Worlds*, Harcourt Brace and Jovanovich, p. 13
137 *The Magician's Nephew*, The Macmillan Company, p. 26
138 Unpublished letter to Arthur Greeves, April 23, 1935
139 *Ibid.*, 1930
140 *Prince Caspian*, The Macmillan Company, pp. 122-123
141 *Letters of C. S. Lewis*, Harcourt Brace and Jovanovich, pp. 71-72

142 Roger Lancelyn Green, *C. S. Lewis*, Henry Z. Walck, Inc., p. 57
143 *Imagination and the Spirit*, Wm. B. Eerdmans Publishing Company, p. 312
144 *Surprised by Joy*, Harcourt Brace and Jovanovich, p. 156
145 Unpublished letter to Arthur Greeves, July 24, 1917
146 *Letters to an American Lady*, Wm. B. Eerdmans Publishing Company, p. 60
147 *Ibid.*, p. 30
148 *Of Other Worlds*, Harcourt Brace and Jovanovich, p. 8
152 *Letters of C. S. Lewis*, Harcourt Brace and Jovanovich, p. 234
156 *Ibid.*, p. 63
157 *Ibid.*, pp. 114-115
158 Unpublished letter to Arthur Greeves, 1915
160 *Surprised by Joy*, Harcourt Brace and Jovanovich, pp. 77-78
161 *The Horse and His Boy*, The Macmillan Company, pp. 68, 70
162 Unpublished letter to Arthur Greeves, #126, June 15, 1930
163 *The Four Loves*, Harcourt Brace and Jovanovich, p. 39
164 *The Horse and His Boy*, The Macmillan Company, p. 16
165 *Letters of C. S. Lewis*, Harcourt Brace and Jovanovich, p. 69
166 *The Four Loves*, Harcourt Brace and Jovanovich, p. 37
167 *Surprised by Joy*, Harcourt Brace and Jovanovich, p. 182
168 Unpublished letter to Arthur Greeves, 1933
169 *Ibid.*
170 *Ibid.*
171 *Ibid.*
172 *Reflections on the Psalms*, Harcourt Brace and Jovanovich, p. 77
173 Unpublished letter to Arthur Greeves, October 1, 1934
175 *Letters to Malcolm*, Harcourt Brace and Jovanovich, pp. 17-18
176 Unpublished account by Dr. Robert E. Havard
177 *Prince Caspian*, The Macmillan Company, p. 50
178 Unpublished letter to Arthur Greeves, January 10, 1931
179 *The Lion, the Witch and the Wardrobe*, The Macmillan Company, pp. 147-148
180 *Ibid.*, p. 105
181 *Letters to an American Lady*, Wm. B. Eerdmans Publishing Company, p. 116
182 *Letters of C. S. Lewis*, Harcourt Brace and Jovanovich, p. 3
184 Roger Lancelyn Green, *C. S. Lewis*, Henry Z. Walck, Inc., p. 23
185 *Light on C. S. Lewis*, Harcourt Brace and Jovanovich, pp. 117-118
186 *Imagination and the Spirit*, Wm. B. Eerdmans Publishing Company, p. 312
188 Unpublished letter by W. H. Lewis